THE ONE THING NECESSARY

The Transforming Power of Christian Love

Leonard Doohan

PUBLICATIONS

Dedication

For Paula

THE ONE THING NECESSARY
The Transforming Power of Christian Love
by Leonard Doohan

Edited by Gregory F. Augustine Pierce
Cover design by Tom A. Wright
Cover art "The Four Evangelists" drawn by Rudolf Koch (1876-1934) from the
book *Christian Symbols* (San Francisco: Arion Press, 1996).
Text design and typesetting by Patricia A. Lynch

Scripture quotations are from the *New Revised Standard Version of the Bible*, copyright © 1989 by the Division of Christian Education of the National Council of the
Churches of Christ in the USA. Used with permission. All rights reserved.

Copyright © 2012 by Leonard Doohan

Published by ACTA Publications, 4848 N. Clark Street, Chicago, IL 60640, (800)
397-2282, www.actapublications.com

Library of Congress Catalogue Number: 2012944506
ISBN: 978-0-87946-492-9
Printed in the United States of America by Versa Press
Year 25 24 23 22 21 20 19 18 17 16 15 14 13 12
Printing 20 19 18 17 16 15 14 13 12 11 10 9 8 7 6 5 4 3 2 First

CONTENTS

*A*t a critical point in his life, Jesus gave to each of us an extraordinary challenge: "A new commandment I give to you, that you also love one another; even as I have loved you, that you also love one another. By this all...will know that you are my disciples, if you have love for one another" (John 13:34-35). Nowadays, we live in a world that is filled with indifference, prejudice, and hatred, and Jesus' hope that Christians would become a prophetical presence of transforming love is more needed than ever. Jesus has called each of us to believe in the power of love, and to let this love motivate us in all we do.

The first reason we believe in love is because each of us has personally experienced God's love toward us. A faith-filled experience of God's love changes our lives, showing us what God has done and continues to do for us and how we ought to respond by modeling our lives on God's love. Living our faith in love is a spiritual journey of discovery, a pilgrimage in which each of us gains a deeper knowledge of God's self-communication to us. It clarifies our relationship to God, the meaning of life, and what our own response to God ought to be. Spiritual writers frequently describe our spiritual journey as a journey of faith. However, the way of faith is simply a preparation for the way of love, and this book challenges all of us to focus our entire lives on the essential call to believe in the power of love.

We all yearn to know the meaning of life, our place in the universe, and the purpose of our existence. What we are really yearning for is love; for this alone satisfies our restlessness. We value love when we see it, we long for it when it is not present, we know it seems to manifest what is the best in us.

We need to acknowledge that love is the central experience that gives meaning to our lives. Why should this be so? I think we value love so much because God has made us this way. God is love and has placed a seed of divine life in each of us. The Trinity is a relationship of love that is dynamic and ever extending itself. Creation is a reaching out of a loving God to increase love through others. Creation is a project of love.

The early Christian disciples were overwhelmed by the emphasis on love in Jesus' extraordinary teachings. They were convinced that love is the kernel of the Christian revelation. However, when we look at our contemporary world this central message of Christianity has never been more needed—or more forgotten—than it is now. This is a time when we Christians can have a prophetical impact on our world by proclaiming the transformational power of love. By our lack of love we frequently turn the world into a kingdom of darkness, sin, and hate, which flows from a failure to love. Hardheartedness, prejudice, bigotry, and hatred are increasing everywhere, and those of us dedicated to God must take note less we lose the battle for the direction of this world. The hate-filled of this world are far better organized than we who seek a reign of love.

We Christians need to renew our commitment to the essentials of love. We must live our lives based on the decision to love and an asceticism that stresses love alone. Perhaps only a few of us will initially accept the challenge of this renewal of our faith in love, but the power of Christian love will percolate up through every level of community interaction until it affects the larger communal expressions of civic and ecclesial life. Our goal is to become channels of divine love. This is the only way to renew ourselves, our Church, and the world. This is our new destiny, and the only way we will find meaning in life.

Jesus told Martha that only one thing is necessary (see Luke 10:41-42). That one thing is love. This book is a call for us to leave aside the many secondary aspects of Christianity and focus our dedication on the single issue that is clearly more important than any other...and than all others put together.

If Christians are to be the leavening presence in the world for which Jesus hoped and prayed, then we must redirect all our lives to focus on the way of love. Let us direct our entire commitment on the call to love. Where needed, let us even revise our ideas on what it even means to be a Christian.

Love's Call

FINDING MEANING IN GOD'S LOVE

*I gave him intellect so that he could recognize and understand
my will in the wisdom of my Son; for it is I who am the source
of all graces, and I burn with a father's love. I also gave him
his will to love, letting him share in the love of the Holy Spirit
so that he could love whatever his intellect had seen and
recognized.*

Catherine of Siena, *On Divine Providence*

*Help us on this day of rest to see goodness in all your creatures;
open our eyes and our hearts to your love in the world.*

Psalter, Week 2, Sunday, "Morning Prayer," Intercessions

*Late have I loved you, O Beauty so ancient and so new; late
have I loved you! For behold you were within me, and I outside;
and I sought you outside and in my ugliness fell upon those
lovely things that you have made. You were with me and I was
not with you. I was kept from you by those things, yet had they
not been in you, they would not have been at all. You called and
cried to me and broke open my deafness...you touched me, and I
have burned for your peace.*

Augustine of Hippo, *Confessions, Book 7*

*Love alone can unify living beings so as to complete and fulfill
them, for it alone joins them by what is deepest in themselves.
All we need is to imagine our ability to love developing until it
embraces the totality of the people of the Earth.*

Teilhard de Chardin, "Meditation"

FOCUS FOR THIS CHAPTER

We human beings are restless and unfulfilled until we rest in God's love.

- *Savor the restlessness we often feel in our search for the meaning of our life.*

- *Answer Jesus' question, "What are you looking for?"*

- *Think about our ordinary and extraordinary experiences of human love and what they tell us about God's love for us.*

- *Explore the spirituality of love.*

- *Reflect on how we come to know God and what God wants for us.*

When I attended high school, many years ago, the motto of the school was *Sicut Cervus* ("as a deer"). These are the first two words of Psalm 42, and they describe a Levite's longing to experience God. These words, and the group of nine psalms (40-49) of which they are a part, present a wonderful image of a believer's search for answers to the most important questions of life's meaning, purpose, and end.

> *As a deer longs for flowing streams,*
> *so my soul longs for you, O God.*
> *My soul thirsts for God,*
> *for the living God.*
> *When shall I come and behold*
> *The face of God?*
>
> Psalm 42:1-2

This psalm certainly portrays a believer's longing to understand and experience God, but it is actually a lament, rather than a joyful assurance of answers, to the yearnings the psalmist feels. In fact, he says later in the psalm, "tears have been my food." People taunt him with the criticism, "Where is your God?" He says his soul is cast down and disquieted, and he even turns to God with the cry, "Why have you forgotten me?" So, he goes about mournfully, oppressed by some and taunted by others.

This block of nine psalms presents the persevering faith of all believers and our longing to be near God—in spite of daily issues that pull us away from this commitment and in spite of the ridicule of others who claim the search itself is a waste of time. The psalmist knows that our search for fulfillment in life is satisfied only in our real experience of God.

The Fathers of the Church described a human being as "a spiritual person" (*homo spiritualis*), and also as "capable of God" (*capax Dei*). We are, as far as we know, the only creatures capable of seeking our own fulfillment and thinking about ultimate values. Our primary tasks as human beings are not merely to survive or procreate but to seek meaning and value in life and, even more, to catch glimpses of who and how God is for us. This yearning is a noble vocation of all humans. It is something within us but greater than we are, a call we simply cannot ignore.

In fact, we cannot get away from it. As Saint Augustine concluded, "Our hearts are restless until they rest in God" (*Confessions, Book 7*). This longing for God is not something abstract, for we are always longing to understand who God is in relation to our own humanity. It is really a yearning to understand the meaning of life itself, a form of longing for self-understanding and self-fulfillment.

All of us in our own way have responded to this call for meaning and fulfillment in the many experiences of life: in high school, college, or university; in relationships, such as friendship, dating, marriage, and family life; in work or in ministry; in organizations and institutions, both civic and ecclesiastical. These profound experiences, lived with dedication and fidelity, bring us closer to God. They give us nothing more than a taste of divinity and then leave us dissatisfied.

Because of the many obstacles to meaning we encounter in our daily life, our search is often as fruitless as the psalmist's, whom we join in a shared lament. Our soul is cast down within us, we journey helplessly, feeling at times forgotten and cast aside, derided and scorned in our pursuit, a laughingstock among the peoples, and covered with a deep darkness (see Psalm 42-49).

I personally find that our times are often as sad to live in as were the psalmist's. Our world seems often to work against our efforts to both understand and experience the divine life that we somehow know is there at all times. Our search for personal fulfillment is essential to the quality of our life, yet it often appears just beyond our grasp.

Yet while the search for God is not easy, it is the daily expression of our hope and the only way to satisfy our deepest yearnings as human beings. And here is the good news: Our successful search for fulfillment lies merely in our open and genuine response to God's ongoing call to experience God's love. Our ultimate meaning is only a love away, and that love is freely available at all times to all people.

In John's Gospel, Jesus appears on the scene and disciples make religious proclamations to one another about him. Jesus does not say anything until later, and then the first words he utters to his disciples speak to us as well: "What are you looking for?" (John 1:38). Our response to that question is a lifelong journey to discover who God is for us.

But how is that yearning going to be satisfied today? I say it is with whatever aids are available, new and old. It may be through the Church or other faiths; it may be through books or films or on the Internet; it could be a song or a sunrise, a birth or a death, something ordinary or extraordinary.

Whatever means we use, we must continue to look at our lives and penetrate to the center of our very existence to find both our true selves and a call to a deeper relationship with God. Our journey to God, to fulfillment, and to union in love is a struggle, as Saint Paul pointed out to the Athenians: God gives all people opportunities "so that they would search for God and perhaps grope for him and find him—though indeed he is not far from each one of us. For 'In him we live and move and have our being'" (Acts 17:27-28). This journey to God requires vision, motivation, often a guide, and the helpful experiences of travelers who have preceded or accompany us.

This is a journey to become the best people we are capable of being. In a world where we modern men and women have mastered everything except ourselves and our own purpose in life, this journey is for those of us who are no longer satisfied with the childish beliefs of the past but yearn to be fully human in our relationship to others and to God. We want to react to the depersonalizing of modern life, to what we see as a diminished sense of the human vocation.

We also want an adult relationship with God. As St. Paul pointed out to the Corinthians, "When I was a child I spoke like a child, I thought like a child, I reasoned like a child; when I became an adult, I put an end to childish ways. For now we see in a mirror, dimly, but then we will see face to face. Now I know only in part; then I will know fully, even as I have been known" (1 Corinthians 13:8-13).

This journey to discover God's ways in our life is an experience that impacts, convinces, and transforms us. It is the courageous journey of grasping our own uniqueness and of pursuing the ultimate meaning of human existence. This journey teaches us that we become more fully human the more we become co-travelers with one another and with a loving God, immersed in God's purpose and grace. This is our destiny and mission in life.

Disciples who undertake this uncommon journey are people who hope and long to become something they are not yet. Such "true" disciples are visionaries, striving for a greater understanding of the purpose of human existence and of God's call. This is a journey for those of us who have found our own emptiness, for it is on a road that can only be followed after we have already lost our way while searching in other directions.

Once begun, this journey has a power and a force all its own, an internal dynamism that keeps us going and focused on values that enthuse and continue to motivate us. Our journey to self-understanding and to a greater experience of God's love begins with simple questions. Why are we the way we are? Why is our world the way it is? Why do we long for something we never seem to attain? What makes us proud of our humanity or ashamed of our humanity?

As we journey, we find the generosity and goodness of many people impress us very positively. In fact, we quickly realize that the people we admire most are those who are known for their love, not their wealth or their skill or their power. It is not that we do not appreciate greatness, creativity, and artistic brilliance, but love is different. Why is it that we humans appreciate love so much when we give or receive it? Is it because love is a manifestation of what is deepest within us, most like what we know we need to be?

Is it not true that we find humans without love to be stunted in their maturing? Failure to love is an abuse that creates a humanity that needs healing (or in Christian terms, redemption). The good news is that on our journey toward meaning and fulfillment love will have a pre-eminent role. The journey to God is an expression of our poverty of spirit that opens us to the love that brings fulfillment.

As Christians, our journey to our fulfillment as human beings is a journey to a deeper understanding of the centrality of love in our lives. Christian spirituality, then, is our search for this love and our way of striving for a greater share in God's existence. Our spirituality is rooted in a faith experience but brings that faith to birth in the ever-changing circumstances of modern life. Our pursuit of this goal of making love the central feature of our spirituality must permeate every aspect of life.

Christian spirituality today stresses the inner journey to self-discovery. Deep within each one of us there is a zone that is naturally divine, where we encounter ourselves searching for love and in the process encounter the God of Love searching for us. Thus, spirituality gives meaning to our very existence.

We can try to build our spirituality on other people's ideas and teachings and these can help motivate us for a while, but eventually there has to be a personal experience that motivates all that we do. The former is a belief system; the latter is a faith-filled experience that is simple, intuitive, passive, indescribable, and transforming. Belief is an articulation, an explanation of our faith. Beliefs change, however, and ought to, as our cultural and historical circumstances change. Faith, on the other hand, is a constant. Those of us with real faith know we have experienced something that has changed everything and that our life can never be the same again. We have caught a glimpse of the meaning of life, at least for ourselves.

This faith-filled experience could be the moment we first discover

that we are loved; or when we feel the unconditional dedication of another; or when we realize that some friendships endure for a lifetime,
even though they are not always the ones we thought would. It could
be the existential moment when we become aware of our own peren-
nial inclination to sin; or a time when everything we previously valued
is lost or taken away. It could be in the awareness of our own need to
continually struggle for something that is not yet within our reach or
the moment when we personally appropriated the vision of our religious tradition.

To use a phrase from another context, a genuine faith-filled experience is a dangerous memory, because when we think back to it we
must confront the fact that the experience changed everything about
us and that we can never be the same again. This is frightening, because if we do not change as a result of our faith-filled experience, we
know it will be the greatest betrayal of our life, one that would silence
love, goodness, and hope in our life forever.

Generally, those of us who have had a profound spiritual experience such as this can remember exactly where we were at the time,
what we were doing, and all the details of the moment. With this experience comes an awareness of its importance in our life: "Guard the
good treasure entrusted to you, with the help of the Holy Spirit living
in us" (2 Timothy 1:14).

This faith-filled experience is always an experience of the otherness of
God. It is not simply an indication about humanity's goodness without
God. Rather, it is a glimpse of a transcendent being that is healing, loving, and unifying. The good news is that in the midst of the turmoil of
this world, love still breaks through.

In fact, we often talk about "faith" and "truth" when speaking of
religion, but for Christians our faith is in the essential truth that love
takes priority over all else. Our experience of spirituality is always at
once an awesome insight into transcendence and otherness in the
midst of our emptiness and helplessness. When considering this experience of love, I am reminded of the words of Kahlil Gibran: "And think

not that you can guide the course of love, for love, if it finds you worthy, will guide your course." As Christians, our search for fulfillment, our journey to God, our experience of faith, all converge in an appreciation of the centrality of love.

Frequently our experience of transcendent love starts with an ordinary event or encounter that either confirms the value of love or cries out for the healing presence of love. In either case, these simple, intuitive experiences are glimpses into transcendent love. We have faith in this experience, but it is not a simple understanding or explanation that results from our reflection on a particular event. Rather, we know we have touched something that we have never touched before. It is beyond understanding, reflection, and interpretation. We recognize it for what it is: an awareness of reality beyond the normal horizons of our life.

After this, every small gesture or denial of love is only understandable against the backdrop of this transcendent love we have experienced. For example, knowing we are loved unconditionally by someone else only has meaning in the context of God's unconditional love. Likewise, hatred and unforgiving responses can only be judged in the context of God's pure love and universal forgiveness. Even in our daily acts of loving or of being loved we witness mystery, and we are at once aware that we "cannot guide the course of love."

Our Christian spiritual journey is a journey of discovery of the transforming value of love. Our love of God and God's love for us gives meaning and value to all our other loving. And as we learn to love others, we learn to love ourselves more.

Of course, our human awareness of God is very limited and rarely amounts to more than the awareness of the existence of a mystery beyond normal horizons. Prior to appreciating and experiencing this mystery beyond normal horizons, we have to purify our previous limiting knowledge of God.

Mystics who have caught glimpses of God say that we encounter God through "unknowing" rather than through "knowing." By this they give us two reminders. One, we need to get rid of all previous images we may have accumulated about God, because God is not like any of the images we have. Abandoning these images is a form of *unknowing*. Two, we will not gain greater insight into God through the exercise of the intellect (knowing) but only through love-filled faith (unknowing). If the former instructs us that God is nothing like we thought God was, the latter instructs us that God never seems to act towards us in the way we thought God would.

So, our awareness of the mystery of love has two rhythms, one theoretical and the other visceral. Both are part of God's call, felt in our own being, in our yearnings, in our spiritual search, and in our profoundest experiences. The good news is that our God of Love is seeking to reveal in us and to us that this world is created for love and sustained by love and that loving relationships with others and with God are central to our lives. This vision of the importance and power of love is the core of God's call to each and every one of us.

QUESTIONS FOR DISCUSSION
FOR PERSONAL REFLECTION ···

1. *Describe what you consider your overriding purpose in life. Where did it come from? How does it relate to love?*

2. *What are three ordinary experiences of love in your life? Did they reveal to you the transcendent nature of God's love for you? Explain. How do you react to the idea of a "spirituality of love"?*

3. *How do you understand the difference between "belief" and "faith"? Which is more visceral and which more theoretical for you? Why? Do you encounter God more with "knowing" or "unknowing"? Give examples.*

Love's Way

JESUS' LIFE OF LOVE FOR HUMANITY

Let us bear in mind too how great is the love God has shown us, since he has given us in Christ such a pledge of that love which he has for us; for love calls for a return of love.

Teresa of Avila, *Autobiography*

People who have righteousness in their hearts—that is they love God—have no need for written prohibitions.

When this righteousness and love towards God were forgotten... God was compelled by his deep love...to reveal himself.

Irenaeus, *Against the Heresies*

Where true love is dwelling, God is dwelling there;
Love's own loving presence love does ever share.
Love of Christ has made us out of many one;
In our midst is dwelling God's eternal Son.
Give him joyful welcome, love him and revere;
Cherish one another with a love sincere.

Hymn, *Office of readings*, Week 4, Thursday

You wake from dreams of doom and—for a moment—you know: beyond all the noise and the gestures, the only real thing, love's calm unwavering flame in the half-light of an early dawn.

Dag Hammarskjold, *Markings*, 29/7/58

FOCUS FOR THIS CHAPTER ··

God gave us Christ,
whose love through death
our ransom paid.

- *Center our reflections on the revelation of the nature of God we received by the Word becoming a human being in the person of Jesus of Nazareth.*

- *Look at how all four evangelists put love at the center of Jesus' teachings.*

- *Analyze how love reacts in specific situations by looking at how Jesus reacted.*

- *Recognize that love trumps law every time they are in conflict.*

- *Consider how our lives ought to be different because of Jesus' challenge to us.*

Whether we humans describe it as searching for personal fulfillment, seeking meaning in life, or trying to experience transcendence, all our efforts lead us to a deeper awareness of the centrality of love in human development. There is no other true place we can end up.

What we are really yearning for is the life of God, which is nothing other than a life of love. And although we think we are journeying to God, it is actually God who is journeying to us to bring us this gift. In arguably the best-known passage in the Bible, one of the early Christian writers put it this way: "For God so loved the world that he gave his only Son, so that everyone who believes in him might not perish but might have eternal life" (John 3:16).

Notice that John did not say "everlasting" life or "never-ending" life or "immortality." He said "eternal" life. Eternal life, by definition, is life that has no end, but it also has no beginning. It is always there. Always has been. Always will be. It is time-less. It is the life of God. It is the life of love. And we get to enter into it. Right now.

We turn in this chapter to consider the coming of this "Son of God" into the world. What did early disciples believe Jesus' purpose to be? When they wrote the gospels, what did *they* take as the focal point of his mission? They included many stories that seem to be unusual for such a significant religious leader—stories that became disclosure episodes of what really were Jesus' priorities. Leaving for the following chapter Jesus' teachings on love, let's focus here on the general picture of his coming and his ministry and see that the central issue of Jesus' entire life and mission was to reveal God's unconditional love for humanity—and for each and every human being.

Matthew announces the coming of Jesus by telling us that the Holy Spirit hovered over Mary as the Spirit of God hovered over the Ark of the Covenant, indicating the presence of God in Jesus from his very conception.

Matthew tells us that the symbolic name of Jesus is "Emmanuel," which means "God is with us." He ends his gospel with the words of Jesus himself: "And remember, I am with you always, to the end of the age" (Matthew 28:20), thereby forming brackets around his entire narrative—a technique implying Matthew's conviction that the God of love is now present to us in a very intimate way.

Luke also emphasizes the overshadowing of Mary with the presence and power of God, but then goes on to present Jesus' coming in a way that reminds us of Greek plays in which characters' names form part of the story-plot. In order of appearance the characters are: Zechariah, whose name means "God has remembered;" Elizabeth, "God is fullness;" John, "God is gracious," Mary, "the beloved;" Joseph, "God gathers together;" and Jesus, "salvation." Luke reminds us that God is full of love for us, graciously offers this divine love to us, treats each of us as a specially loved child, gathers us together in a community of love, and in these ways brings all of humanity salvation. At Jesus' birth Luke adds a telling detail: Mary placed the child in a manger. This shepherd loves his flock so much he becomes food for us all.

All three Synoptic Gospels (Matthew, Mark, Luke) narrate Jesus' baptism by John, the presence of the Holy Spirit in the form of a dove, and the voice of the Father proclaiming Jesus his beloved Son. This Trinitarian epiphany, the consecration of Jesus for his life's work, stresses that he comes as the fulfillment of God's love for the world.

Before the public ministry of Jesus begins, however, both Matthew and Luke tell us that Jesus was tempted by selfishness, power, and glory. He was human, after all. Yet, unlike us, each time he refused the temptations of self-love, knowing that the love of the Father that he had experienced was not for him alone but for every person who lived, had lived, or would live on the earth. To drive home this point, Luke repeats these same three temptations when Jesus hangs on the cross, but Jesus rejects them once again, for his love of humanity is irrevocable.

Mark and Matthew both present Jesus' first words as: "The time is fulfilled, and the kingdom of God has come near; repent and believe in the good news" (Mark 1:15; Matthew 4:17). Here the word "repent" means undergoing a change of heart, gaining an entirely new outlook on life, finding a new way of love. This idea of a radical new beginning is also seen in Luke's presentation of Jesus' inaugural "sermon" in his hometown of Nazareth, in which Jesus, echoing the great Hebrew prophet Isaiah, specifies his ministry of loving care for all in need, in the final "Jubilee" (which means "to raise a joyful shout") year that has begun with his coming.

Jesus sees himself as the path to the God of love. He sees his mission as inaugurating "the Kingdom of God," a new and final period of world history when people will look at the world from a totally different perspective: the law of love.

Several times in his ministry in the Synoptics, Jesus points out the reason for his coming into the world. In the Gospel of Mark, after calling Levi, a man who earned his living by extortion, Jesus dines with him and others who were known for their abuse of others and for their self-love. When the Pharisees challenge Jesus for being in such people's presence, Jesus replies "I have come to call not the righteous but sinners" (Mark 2:17), and in Matthew Jesus adds, echoing the prophet Hosea, "Go and learn what this means, 'I desire mercy, not sacrifice'" (Matthew 9:13).

Jesus later points out that part of his mission is to gather together a new family for God. Following a series of miracles, Jesus tells a man whom he has healed, "Go home to your friends, and tell them how much the Lord has done for you and what mercy he has shown to you" (Mark 5:19).

In an unusual episode, Matthew presents Jesus saying, "Do not think that I have come to bring peace to the earth; I have not come to bring peace, but a sword" (Matthew 10:34). In this episode, Jesus presents himself as a sign of contradiction who, without wanting discord and division, finds that the demands of his way of love, relentlessly pursued, provoke negative reactions in many people.

Isn't this still the case today? Many in every generation remain unconvinced that pursuing the way of love is the best path for them.

They find money and power and violence more conducive to obtaining their dreams of happiness.

Jesus contrasts these people with his true disciples in every age, of whom he says, "I thank you, Father, Lord of heaven and earth, because you have hidden these things from the wise and the intelligent and have revealed them to infants" (Matthew 11:25-27). He goes on to insist that the Father entrusted everything to him and that no one knows the ways of the Father except him. What is that way? Love. Love. And more love.

Jesus ends this dissertation in Matthew with what many spiritual writers call the most comforting passage of the New Testament: "Come to me, all you that are weary and are carrying heavy burdens, and I will give you rest. Take my yoke upon you, and learn from me; for I am gentle and humble in heart, and you will find rest for your souls. For my yoke is easy and my burden is light" (Matthew 11:28-30).

Luke's Gospel offers a similar idea at the end of Jesus' visit to Zacchaeus' home: "For the Son of Man came to seek out and to save the lost" (Luke 19:10). Jesus' enduring love for his disciples motivates him in all he does. Later, following some disciples' dispute over who was the greatest, Jesus insisted the way his own ministry needed to be: "But I am among you as one who serves" (Luke 22:27).

When we see and comprehend Jesus' insatiable love for us, we must conclude that what we see is beyond normal human horizons and gives us insight into the way God would have things.

It seems that Jesus was aware throughout his life that he would be put to death for his unambiguous and unrelenting commitment to love as the only way that the human race could survive and thrive: "I came that they may have life, and have it abundantly" (John 10:10). Nothing seemed to deter him from "going to Jerusalem," which he somehow knew would be where it would happen.

His death would be a direct consequence of those in power's hatred of God's way of love, and Jesus certainly would not change his approach. He suffered because he loved so much, indicating the foundation of the way of love for all Christians. Jesus was condemned to the cross by those who rejected love, and he accepted the cross because of his irrevocable dedication to love: "Christ also suffered for you, leaving you an example, so that you would follow in his steps" (1 Peter 2:21).

Again anticipating his death, he praised the woman with the alabaster jar who anointed him and later predicted that one of his closest disciples, to whom he had shown so much love, would betray him. Jesus gave himself to his disciples in the ritual he gave us at the Last Supper, a way of being close not only to him but also to all his disciples.

The insights into Jesus' mission of love coming from the Synoptic Gospels are complemented by John's approach to Jesus' ministry and destiny: "The word came from the Father, filled with enduring love.... And of this fullness we have all been given a share, love in place of love" (John 1:14-15, translation by Raymond Brown).

These verses from the beginning of John's gospel indicate that Jesus comes to us filled with the Father's love and brings us a new kind of love, different from all previous understandings.

Apparently a lot of people who encountered Jesus experienced his love and his challenge to love. The Evangelist John, who was obviously overwhelmed by this experience of love, writes in one of his short letters:

> *Beloved, let us love one another, because love is from God; everyone who loves is born of God and knows God. Whoever does not love does not know God, for God is love. God's love was revealed among us in this way: God sent his only Son into the world so that we might live through him. In this is love, not that we loved God but that he loved us and sent his Son to be the atoning sacrifice for our sins. Beloved, since God loved us so much, we also ought to love one another. No one has ever seen God; if we love one another, God lives in us, and his love is perfected in us.*

> 1 John 4:7-12

Written around 90-100 C.E., just sixty years after Jesus' death, these words could be a synopsis of the entre Christian creed, simple and powerful, essential and challenging. Jesus, who in Christian spiritual writings is often referred to as "the beloved" or "the lover," is a gift to us of the Father's love, he comes to us as the embodiment of love, and his life of love for us is the model of a new way of living in this world. Love's life is the example for us to follow.

In John's Gospel, Jesus gathers his disciples with the question, "What are you looking for?" and he says to them "Come and see" (John 1:38-39). From early in his ministry, Jesus knows the mission that lies ahead and knows his part in it. "The Father loves the Son and has placed all things in his hands" (John 3:35; 5:20). He has brought the Father's love to the world. "My teaching is not mine but his who sent me" (John 7:16). In fact, he can simply say, "I declare what I have seen in the Father's presence" (John 8:38), and even more profoundly, "The Father and I are one" (John 10:30). Jesus knows his purpose is to bring the Father's love to the world.

Jesus describes himself this way in another famous passage in the Gospel of John: "I am the way, and the truth, and the life. No one comes to the Father except through me. If you know me, you will know my Father also. From now on you do know him and have seen him" (John 14:6).

In John's Gospel, people throughout the world must take a stand in view of the Father's love made visible in Jesus. Their love or non-love is what judgment is all about. To those who love he says, "The Father himself loves you, because you have loved me and have believed that I came from God" (John 16:27). To those who live in non-love Jesus says. "Yet you refuse to come to me to have life" (John 5:40). At the end of his great prayer at the Last Supper, Jesus speaks to the Father concerning those who follow him, "As you, Father, are in me and I am in you, may they also be in us, so that the world may believe that you have sent me" (John 17:21).

Glancing at the gospels, then, we see that all four of the evangelists identify love as the very reason for Jesus' coming, the center of his purpose, the reason for his actions, including his death and resurrection.

His mission was to inaugurate in his very person a "Kingdom of Love" and form a community of his own followers dedicated to God's way of love. This is the kernel of the experience of the followers of Jesus throughout the ages.

Love's way is perhaps best seen in the small episodes of Jesus' ministry, where he appears as a very loving and compassionate person. Jesus is the embodiment of the reality of God's love, even in the simple events of every day. Jesus is very human, compassionate, and full of love and care for the poor and the outcasts. Although religions are never without rules and laws, Jesus always gives priority to people's needs over laws.

The gospels stress the compassion of Jesus in all kinds of situations. Jesus acknowledges that the most important commandment of all was to give oneself to God with total love. Then he adds that the second commandment was similar to the first—to love one's neighbor.

Jesus certainly evidences this love throughout his ministry. When healing people, he obviously wants to help them out of their misery. When faced with large crowds, "he had compassion for them, because they were harassed and helpless, like sheep without a shepherd" (Matthew 9:36). Before the feeding of the five thousand, the evangelist tells us, "When he went ashore, he saw a great crowd; he had compassion for them and cured their sick" (Matthew 14:14). Before the feeding of the four thousand, Jesus says, "I have compassion for the crowd, because they have been with me now for three days and have nothing to eat; and I do not want to send them away hungry, for they might faint on the way" (Matthew 15:32).

Jesus is also very thoughtful in the small concerns of everyday life. Maybe he got this from his mother, who insisted that he perform his first miracle over something as mundane as having enough wine for a wedding feast. He expresses concern that the little children not be scandalized, urges his apostles to let the children come to him, and lifts them up to bless them. When he notices that his disciples are tired, he says, "Come away to a deserted place all by yourselves and rest a while" (Mark 6:31).

Human beings show their innermost feelings through their bodies. God's love for the world is seen in the fact that the Son takes on human form to share our life. Likewise in his ministry Jesus shows human feelings and at times strong emotions. The evangelist Mark points these out to us, even though later writers tend to omit them. The Markan Jesus is full of compassion and is "moved with pity" (Mark 1:41) at the sight of an approaching leper. He is delighted to put his arms around the children and express his love for the rich young man's life of dedication.

When Pharisees watched to see if Jesus would heal a man with a withered hand on the Sabbath, Jesus "looked around at them with anger; he was grieved at their hardness of heart" (Mark 3:5). The lack of faith of the Nazarenes distresses him. Later, when the Pharisees test him again, he is truly disturbed, and "he sighed deeply in his spirit" (Mark 8:12). When his good friend Lazarus dies, Jesus weeps like any other human being. He feels for people with genuine love.

Jesus' love finds expression in his frequent contacts with the outcasts and the poor. Jesus welcomes the poor, the diseased, and the possessed, who are all shunned by the community. Shunning the poor is never God's way. The Apostle James tells us in his Letter, "Has not God chosen the poor in the world to be rich in faith and to be heirs of the kingdom that he has promised to those who love him?" (James 2:5). Jesus claims to bring glad tidings to the poor and liberty, recovery, and release to the needy. His beatitudes praise the situations of the poor and oppressed. When questioned by the disciples of John the Baptist, he replies that they should tell John what Jesus does for the blind, the lame, lepers, the deaf, and even those who have died, and then John will understand.

When Jesus describes the last judgment, the criteria for judgment are acts of mercy and love, not following the rules. Many of his miracles benefit the poor and oppressed: the possessed whom society shuns and fears; the leper, who must publicly proclaim himself unclean; the paralyzed and helpless; the woman with the hemorrhage that makes her ritually unclean; the widow of Nain, who having lost her only son is without relatives in a society that considers that state a curse; the sinful woman who prostitutes herself; and Jairus' daughter, dead at twelve, the age her society recognized as the beginning of womanhood.

Jesus seems to deliberately choose direct involvement with the outcasts of the society of his day and shows them abundant love. After he calls Levi, he dines with him and some of his friends and coworkers. When the Pharisees criticize Jesus for this, he replies, "I have come to call not the righteous but sinners to repentance" (Luke 5:32). Jesus appeals to tax collectors, and they respond enthusiastically to him. Another group of outcasts in Jesus' day were Samaritans. Jesus speaks positively of them in the story of the Good Samaritan and points out that the only grateful leper was a Samaritan.

Then there were public sinners with whom no one wanted to associate. Jesus courageously reaches out to these; the sinful woman, Zacchaeus, and the good thief with whom he was crucified.

Jesus constantly shows concern for people over laws. As the Psalmist said, "The Lord is just in all his ways, and kind in all his doings" (Psalm 145:17). On a number of occasions people challenge Jesus on the importance of laws; he replies insisting that he wants mercy and compassion before any laws. Some Pharisees criticize Jesus' disciples because they did not fast, whereas the disciples of John the Baptist did. Jesus replies that they have every reason to rejoice because they have him with them, and in this case fasting is not necessary.

Later, the Pharisees again criticize the disciples because they gather some grains of corn on the Sabbath, which the Pharisees equate with breaking the Sabbath command against work. Jesus replies by describing episodes in the life of King David to show the importance of human need taking precedence over human made laws. When a Pharisee invites Jesus to dinner, the disciples do not wash their hands before the meal. When the Pharisees criticize them for this, Jesus challenges back on their behalf, pointing out that it is what is inside a person that makes him or her clean or unclean, and not the outsides of cups.

Jesus not only condemns the Pharisees for giving priority to human laws over compassionate care for human need, but sometimes he challenges his disciples too. When the Samaritans refuse Jesus entry into one of their towns, James and John suggest calling down fire from heaven to punish them. Jesus rebukes them and just walks away. When John and James later mention to Jesus that there is a man who is working miracles in Jesus' name without being one of the "official group," the two apostles seem to want to control membership in the leadership group. However, Jesus says, "Do not stop him; for no one who does a deed of power in my name will be able soon afterwards to speak evil of me" (Mark 9:38-41).

Jesus holds little stock in legalism. When others wanted to condemn the woman who anointed Jesus' feet, he simply said, "her sins, which were many, have been forgiven; hence she has shown great love" (Luke 7:47). At a time when religions emphasize sexual sin, Jesus just tells them to leave her alone for she has loved much. In fact he constantly gives priority to people over laws. This is in keeping with the Hebrew Scripture's understanding of God: "The Lord is gracious and merciful, slow to anger, and abounding in steadfast love. The Lord is good to all, and his compassion is over all that he has made" (Psalm 145:8-9).

Clearly the greatest expression of Jesus' love is his acceptance of death on the cross. He dies rather than weaken his own dedication and the clarity of his commitment to enduring love. He is after all the good shepherd. Living for love and dying for love take on new meaning in Jesus. For him, his death was the outcome of a life of progressive love, in which he always chose the most loving thing to do. Throughout his ministry he realized what would be the inevitable end, for there were repeated references to attempted violence against him and a growing intense hostility toward his message. Certainly his death is a source of life: he dies to sin, to human weaknesses, to the legalism of religion. He shows us a love that knows no boundaries, no exceptions—love that accepts all consequences of its own choices. He dies to show what he also showed in each moment of his public life—that our choice must always be for love. For God is love, and Jesus is the revelation of God's perfect love for us all.

Throughout his ministry, Jesus confronts organized religion's neatly packaged claims with the challenge and request to establish a relationship with him: "Come to me" (Matthew 11:28-30). He points out that religious practices are all well and good, but if we wish to be perfect, we need to follow him. Love for Jesus takes precedence over all other relationships; discipleship is a total dedication to him, not to religious teachings. Jesus shows his disciples (us included, of course) throughout the ministry what love looks like, culminating in the notable example of his washing our feet.

An interesting episode takes place in the appendix to John's gospel. This is the only gospel in which Jesus speaks of love for himself. As he walks along the shore of the lake with his resurrected body, he three times says to Simon Peter, "Simon, Son of John, do you love me more than these?" (John 21:15), to which Peter answers, "Lord, you know everything; you know that I love you" (John 21:17). Love is the only thing Jesus wants from us. This is love's way.

QUESTIONS FOR DISCUSSION
FOR PERSONAL REFLECTION ··

1. When Jesus says to you, "Come and see," what is it you want him to show you? Be specific. And creative.

2. What is your vocation? That is, how are you called to incarnate (make real) God's love in the world? How can you do that in your daily life on your job, with your family and loved ones, in your community and civic involvement? What is blocking you: laws, fear, lack of knowledge or support, something else? How can you overcome them?

3. Which simple episode of love in Jesus' life amazes you the most? Why? Who are today's lepers, prostitutes, and tax collectors? Name some of them. What have you done in the past six months to show them that you love them? What can you do in the next six months to do so? Will you? Why or why not?

Love's Word

JESUS' TEACHINGS ON LOVE

*See, dear friends, what a great and wondrous thing love is.
Its perfection is beyond all words. Who is fit to be called its
possessor, but those whom God deems worthy? Let us beg and
implore of his mercy that we may be...found faultless in love.*

Clement I of Rome, *Letter to the Corinthians*

Love conquers all; let us too yield to Love.

Virgil

*And now, my children, listen to me:
happy are those who keep my ways.
Hear instruction and be wise and do not neglect it.
Happy is the one who listens to me.*

Proverbs 8:32-33

*So if there is any encouragement in Christ, any incentive of love,
any participation in the Spirit, any affection and sympathy,
complete my joy by being of the same mind, having the same
love, being in full accord and of one mind.*

Paul, Letter to the Philippians, 2:1-2

FOCUS FOR THIS CHAPTER ⋯⋯⋯⋯⋯⋯⋯⋯⋯⋯⋯⋯

Jesus' teachings insist on love, and we are called to share this love.

- *Become more aware that when the New Testament writers focus on the essential teachings of Jesus, they always start with and come back to love.*

- *Listen to Paul's descriptions of "a still more excellent way," namely love.*

- *Realize the uniqueness of the Christian emphasis on the love of Christ as the path to the Father.*

- *Make the connection between the commandment to love and the fact that our happiness is linked to lives built on love.*

- *Explore how we can make Christian love practical in our troubled world today.*

The very first chronological book in the New Testament is neither one of the gospels or the Acts of the Apostles. It is Paul's letter to the Thessalonians, written about 50-51 C.E., some twenty years after Jesus' death. Think about that. The first piece of canonical writing in the Christian tradition we have wasn't put on paper (actually parchment) until Jesus would have been in his mid-fifties! That would be like someone in 2012 writing for the first time (and without the benefit of a Google search) about something that happened in 1992 (the first election of Bill Clinton as president, say, or the collapse of the Soviet Union).

Yet what had happened to these early Christians was much more important. These people believed that they had encountered the one, true God in the person of a young Jewish man from the backwater region of Galilee, who had been executed by the Romans, had somehow risen from the dead and been seen by many witnesses, and then had left them to be with the One he called his Father in heaven. They had been infused with God's Holy Spirit and given courage to take this man Jesus' message of the Kingdom of God throughout the known world. They faced persecution but also tremendous success in drawing new people, especially Gentiles (non-Jews) and the poor and oppressed, into their movement.

Now they were starting to write down what they had experienced and learned. These documents would be one of their greatest legacies for generations to come. What would they write about? What would they want to make sure others that came after them understood and did not forget?

They would write mostly about love. They would try to explore the depth of Jesus' challenge to love God and to love others. They would give a glimpse into the program for a new way of being human that Jesus proclaimed, a program summarized in a later letter to the Ephesians: "Therefore, be imitators of God, as beloved children, and live in love, as Christ loved and gave himself up for us" (Ephesians 5:1-2).

The first of the writings, however, is a simple letter of sound pastoral advice from a man who was not even one of Jesus' original disciples, a man who never even met Jesus except in a vision on the road to Damascus where the man was heading to lead a persecution of the followers of Jesus. That man's name was Saul, who changed it to Paul when he became what eventually came to be called a "Christian."

Paul's first letter tries to reinforce his initial preaching and give his support to the Christians in the town of Thessalonica in Macedonia. He deals with some concerns they have on moral issues, the end of the world, and life in community. Paul is not dealing with opposition or serious abuses, as he will have to do in later writings to other communities, nor is he presenting a doctrinal synthesis, as he will for example in the letter to the Romans.

Rather, Paul's short letter to the Thessalonians is upbeat, optimistic, and supportive of the new Christians there. As Paul commends the Thessalonians for their "work of faith and labor of love and steadfastness of hope" (1 Thessalonians 1:2), he singles out one quality for special attention and special commendation, a development in the community that gives him pride. "Now concerning love of the brothers and sisters, you do not need anyone to write to you, for you yourselves have been taught by God to love one another; and indeed you do love all the brothers and sisters throughout Macedonia. But we urge you, beloved, to do so more and more" (1 Thessalonians 4:9-10). He then tells them they must make this love practical in their daily work and witnessing to others.

Paul's letter to the Galatians, written around 54 C.E. during Paul's third missionary journey, possibly while he was in Corinth, has a very different tone than that of his letter to the Thessalonians. Some agitators in Galatia have questioned Paul's authority and raised the central issue of the relationship of Christianity to Judaism. Paul takes a radical approach and contrasts the two religious systems that he sees as no longer compatible. Paul is animated, argumentative, and confrontational, as he justifies his own authority, and then he gives six proofs for Christianity's approach to faith in contrast to Judaism's emphasis on the law. He warns the Galatians against turning to "a different gospel" (Galatians 1:6), and perverting the gospel of Christ. Later in the letter, he sets forth his own understanding of the gospel, culminating with his own conviction of God's love for him. "[It] is no longer I who live, but it is Christ who lives in me. And the life I now live in the flesh I live by faith in the Son of God, who loved me and gave himself for me" (Galatians 2:20). This belief in the love of God, who in Christ becomes the source of life for all disciples, is the essence of the gospel that Paul preaches.

Paul's first letter to the Corinthians is an obvious reaction to a lost letter from them asking for clarifications on a series of issues affecting their community life and to some information he had received orally about problems in the community. Paul's letter focuses immediately on the centrality of Christ and then presents a series of arguments on key issues raised in community—on divisions, morality, social status, living in diverse religious environments, liturgical assembly, and the resurrection. Paul deals with these practical problems while also weaving throughout his answers some profound insights on community, ministry, Christian asceticism, the importance of the crucifixion, authentic worship, and resurrection at the end of time. In commenting on the Corinthians' divisive emphasis on their own gifts of knowledge, however, Paul insists the gift he is looking for is love, for "love builds up" (1 Corinthians 8:1).

It is in the midst of all these practical pastoral issues, Paul digresses, and with an enthusiasm bordering on ecstasy says, "I will show you a still more excellent way" (1 Corinthians 12:31). He then launches into his extraordinary hymn to love as the greatest of all spiritual gifts. Paul stresses that love is the measure by which all other gifts in the community should be judged. When Paul wrote to the Galatians, he also listed love as the first of all gifts, but here he seems to see love as something over and above all other gifts, something absolutely essential to being a Christian.

Paul insists that love is more important than anything: speaking in tongues, prophesying, knowledge, voluntary poverty, even martyrdom. None of these have worth without love—partly because they all come to an end, whereas love continues into eternity. He goes on to describe the characteristics of authentic Christian love in this list of attributes:

> *Love is patient;*
> *love is kind;*
> *love is not envious or boastful or arrogant or rude.*
> *It does not insist on its own way;*
> *it is not irritable or resentful;*
> *it does not rejoice in wrongdoing, but rejoices in the truth.*
> *It bears all things, believes all things, hopes all things, endures*
> *all things.*

1 Corinthians 13:4-7

For Paul, love is a sign of Christian maturity; it means a disciple has begun to see Christian values clearly, and to appreciate that love is part of the revelation of God's life that continues in eternity. "Love never ends.... And now faith, hope, and love abide, these three; and the greatest of these is love" (1 Corinthians 13:8, 13).

Paul's main focus is on love of neighbor, but the love of God is also integral to the picture he presents. Paul concludes his letter, "Let all that you do be done in love" (1 Corinthians 16:14).

In the second letter to the Corinthians the atmosphere and mood change sharply, and the focus becomes direct opposition to Paul and personal attacks on him and his apostolic authority. Paul moves from self-defense, to argumentation, and to pleas for reconciliation. In spite of the disagreements he insists on the need for love. "So I urge you to reaffirm your love for him" (2 Corinthians 2:8). Immersed in his own suffering he insists, "For the love of Christ urges us on" (2 Corinthians 5:14). He challenges the Corinthians to "Open wide your hearts" (2 Corinthians 6:13) and calls on them to put all things in order so that "the God of love and peace will be with you" (2 Corinthians 13:11).

Paul writes the letter to the Philippians from prison in Ephesus around 54-57 C.E. He has a warm relationship with the community but writes because of his concerns about dissension within the community and opposition from outside. Although Paul is worried about the Philippians and anxious about his own possible death, the letter is filled with joy and love. He states his hope for them. "And this is my prayer, that your love may overflow more and more with knowledge and full insight to help you determine what is best" (Philippians 1:9-10). Above all he wants their unity and love to grow. "If there is any encouragement in Christ, any consolation from love, any sharing in the Spirit, any compassion and sympathy, make my joy complete: be of the same mind, having the same love, being in full accord and of one mind" (Philippians 2:1-2). He then presents a wonderful hymn describing Christ's humility and selflessness as an example for the Philippians to follow.

The letter to the Romans, often called the "gospel of Paul," is an extended presentation of Paul's understanding of the Good News. Paul sends it around 57-58 C.E. as a self-introduction to the Roman church, which he hopes to visit on his way to Spain. In fact, it becomes his last will and testament. Although he understands something of the Roman situation, he is under no pressure to resolve problems or answer community related questions. Rather, he is free to pause and write his major summary of the Christian faith as he understands it.

The doctrinal part of Romans combines three great themes, and there follows a section on daily life. While dealing with complicated theological arguments, Paul also weaves in his convictions on the love of God as central to the Christian message. He speaks of God's kindness and impartiality and that God has written the divine law in our hearts. He highlights that "God proves his love for us in that while we were still sinners Christ died for us" (Romans 5:8). Paul speaks about reconciliation, liberation, and life in the Spirit and insists that in God's love all who are led by the Spirit of God are children of God, God's beloved.

Paul tells the Romans we are all parts of the same body, and so our love for each other must be genuine; we must love one another with mutual affection, mutual forgiveness, and constant harmony. Then he sums up his views. "Owe no one anything, except to love one another; for the one who loves another has fulfilled the law" (Romans 13:8-10).

For Paul all commandments can be summed up in these words, "Love your neighbor as yourself. Love does no wrong to a neighbor; therefore, love is the fulfillment of the law" (Romans 13:9-10). This is a simple but powerful conclusion to Paul's profound theological tract. In reading Romans it becomes clear that atonement for sin alone is not an adequate motive for the incarnation, for atonement and redemption are part of a larger picture of the primacy of love for all humanity.

As the early Christians gave firm organizational and theological foundations to their belief and religion, the theme of the love of God identified in the love of the Son is placed constantly before our minds and hearts. We have seen this in the four gospels and in the earliest New Testament writer Paul, and the trend continued in other New Testament writers too. The life of love is the eternal life we are given and which we seek. Love is God's way, and we must make it our way too.

The Gospel of John is the only one in which Jesus speaks of love for himself. "If God were your Father, you would love me, for I came from God and now I am here" (John 8:42). Abiding in Jesus' love means keeping his commandments: "They who have my commandments and keep them are those who love me; and those who love me will be loved by my Father, and I will love them and reveal myself to them" (John 14:21).

When Jesus mentions commandments, he is really referring to his way of life, his way of love: "Those who love me will keep my word" (John 14:23). Those who listen to Jesus' word receive eternal life.

The request that disciples abide in the love of Jesus is an extraordinary revelation in world religions; no other religious tradition speaks in this way. It is Jesus' love for us that teaches and leads us to love the Father. We are talking about a revolutionary approach to religion in which the path to God goes through the person of Jesus, not through the temple, church, mosque, or holy site. His disciples' lives focus on developing true love of self, others, the world, and God, and on removing all forms of false love. John's gospel contains no collection of ethical teachings such as those in the other gospels or in Paul, or in the

Hebrew Scriptures or the Koran for that matter. Rather, the authentic response to Jesus' teachings according to John is abiding in the love of the Lord. "And this is his commandment that we should believe in the name of his Son Jesus Christ and love one another, just as he has commanded us. All who obey his commandments abide in him, and he abides in them" (1 John 3:23-24).

Jesus called on disciples to keep his word, and he told them exactly what that meant. "I give you a new commandment, that you love one another. Just as I have loved you, you also should love one another. By this everyone will know that you are my disciples, if you have love for one another" (John 13:34). Later he repeats this and gives his own death for others as a perfect example: "No one has greater love than this, to lay down one's life for one's friends" (John 15:13). Jesus revealed God's love to the world and modeled that love for us. He challenges us to love one another but also prays that we will attain the loving union he wants for us. "Holy Father, protect them in your name that you have given me, so that they may be one, as we are one" (John 17:11). Later he prays "that they may become completely one, so that the world may know that you have sent me and have loved them even as you have loved me" (John 17:23).

Jesus calls us to abide in his love as he abides in the Father's love. The key to abiding in Jesus' love is that we love one another. During the Last Supper, Jesus gives us an example of love in the washing of the feet, and then we hear his final speech in which John tries to catch what he thought were the major teachings of Jesus. For John, Jesus' last will and testament could be no other than Jesus' teachings on love.

The early disciples were well aware of Jesus' challenge to follow the way of love. This way of love is profound but also very practical, for it disdains the judgment of the world and provides detailed strategies for making the world a place where God's love reigns. We see this vision of practical love in Acts, where Luke speaks of the disciples' outreach in justice and peace. Certainly Luke condemns personal sin, but his most forceful condemnations are against injustice and social sin. This evidences the early Church's acute sense of social injustice.

Jesus in his parables condemns social sin: ambition, violence and revenge, greed, possessiveness, dishonesty, and any attitude that ignores the poor. In passing on Jesus' teaching to us, Luke also condemns sexual misconduct, the avoidance of taxes, entrapment, false accusations, and bribery. He knows that sometimes social sin is the normal order of the day in a corrupt society, where public scandal is rampant, greed leads to inheritance litigation, some resort to robbery and mugging, and there is much abuse of power and authority. He sees the evil of materialism, the desire for social acceptance, security at any cost, squandering of wealth, and misuse of other people's property.

Luke is aware of the injustice perpetrated by political institutions, particularly when supported by corrupt judges. He knows of misuse of the pressures of crowds, false accusation, and punishment for the criticism of immoral public figures. He speaks against imprisonment without trial and excessive punishment for what is not even criminal. He knows, too, that religious persecutions are instigated for political or social benefits. The sinful world described by Luke includes slavery, conspiracy to murder, political rivalries, and war.

Even in the area of religion, Luke sees injustice as rampant. Outward religious observance often goes with inner sin and injustice. Religious hypocrisy leads to socially accepted generosity but nothing more. The corrupt and wealthy eventually become impervious to religious values, and others commercialize religion. Luke identifies injustice within religion in the abuse of leadership, false interpretations of Scripture that create intolerable burdens for the people, insistence on the primacy of religious laws over basic human needs, refusal of freedom of conscience, and indifference by religious leaders to injustice.

The situation described by Luke is not unlike our world situation today, as our daily newspapers confirm. This is the arena in which we Christian disciples today must live out the way of love. Jesus did not flee from this unjust world (he could have joined the Essenes in the desert, for example) but deliberately brought the message of the transforming value of love into people's daily lives, using everyday examples, stories, and metaphors with which they would have been very familiar.

The early Christian writers knew love must be lived out in interaction with this sinful world. Jesus' great charter sermon in Luke, paralleling the Sermon on the Mount in Matthew, becomes a challenge to society's values and a reaffirmation of the importance of the poor and oppressed.

Jesus expected rejection from his followers on this point (see the story of the rich young man) and condemned many individuals he met for their possessiveness and lack of concern for the poor. His concern for the poor and his warnings against riches are clear and frequent. For Jesus, then, there is a close link between discipleship and commitment to social reform: "Sell your possessions, and give alms…. For where your treasure is, there your heart will be also" (Luke 12:33-34). Jesus' position was so clear to the early disciples that they established themselves in simple religious communities where they shared all in common and gave away whatever they could to those in need. We don't do that today, but it doesn't lessen the call for us to be good stewards of our possessions and use them to help bring about the kingdom on earth, as it is in heaven.

Dedication to the Lord in faith and love overflows to others in justice and peace. Early followers recognized Jesus as the bringer of peace. When he worked with the needy and brought transformation into their lives, they went away in peace; when they rejected Jesus and his message (that rich young man, Nicodemus, Judas), they lost what peace they had.

Peace is not simply a greeting but what happens when we accept and live the way that Jesus taught. Dedicating ourselves to a life of love for God and for others leads us to peace, but living in self-love means we get no satisfaction from life. Thus, Jesus condemns the rich fool who stores his wealth in silos and reminds everyone, "So it is with those who store up treasures for themselves but are not rich toward God" (Luke 12:21).

The gift of peace that comes with the way of love leads to a way of life fraught with social and political implications, however. The disciple does not react to oppression by others but sees it as part of the conflict that comes with love. Jesus faced a world not unlike ours and sought to transform it little by little into a world of love and peace. The challenge was enormous and cost him his life, but he came to reveal the Father's love to the world and had no choice but to pursue it to its inevitable conclusion. So must we: "Beloved, let us love one another, because love is from God; everyone who loves is born of God and knows God. Who-ever does not love does not know God, for God is love" (1 John 4:7-8).

QUESTIONS FOR DISCUSSION
FOR PERSONAL REFLECTION

1. *Take Paul's list of love's attributes in 1 Corinthians 13:4-7 and rewrite it, substituting the things you believe love is. Share your list with someone. Then revise your list again. Finally, go back and compare your list with Paul's. Revise your list one more time. Now try to live it.*

2. *If love were a crime, would there be enough evidence to convict you? Explain your answer. If Jesus were your "personal life coach" today, what would he ask you to do that you are not doing?*

3. *Justice and peace. Why are they so hard to accomplish? Why are they so controversial? Do you put them off and settle for being "nice" or "charitable" or "not rocking the boat'? What happens when you do—to yourself and to others?*

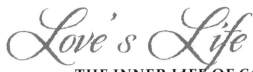

Love's Life

THE INNER LIFE OF GOD IS A LIFE OF LOVE

The lovers of God have no religion but God alone.

Rumi

Life begins and ends with these two qualities. Faith is the beginning, and love is the end; and the union of the two together is God.

Ignatius of Antioch, *Letter to the Ephesians*

Love is the result of love, it is intrinsically valuable. I love because I love; I love in order to love. Love is a valuable thing only if it returns to its beginning, consults its origin and flows back to its source..... When God loves, he wishes only to be loved in return; assuredly he loves for no other purpose than to be loved.

St. Bernard, *Song of Songs*, Sermon 83

Again, love is nothing other than God. God loves himself and his nature, his being and his divinity. In the same love, however, in which God loves himself, he also loves all creatures, not as creatures but he loves the creatures as God. In the same love in which God loves himself, he loves all things.

Meister Eckhart, Sermon 3

FOCUS FOR THIS CHAPTER ···

The three have one love, which is their essence.

- *Remind ourselves that the essence of Christianity is not teachings, laws, or regulations, but rather a personal relationship with God in Christ.*

- *Consider how we can model our own lives on the relationship of love within the Trinity.*

- *Celebrate our new birth as children of God's love.*

- *Appreciate the mystical quality of God's strategy of love and our response to it.*

- *Revisit our ideas on what it means to be Christian—what is essential.*

*F*or the last quarter century, I have used the same chain for my house and car keys. It bears a saying, "In the evening of your life, you will be judged on love." I find it to be a powerful reminder of the most important issue of life.

As a university professor, I have presented courses on a wide variety of topics in Scripture, ecclesiology, and spirituality. I have given hundreds of workshops all over the world on lay ministry, leadership, business ethics, and healthcare. I look at our Christian churches and service institutions today and the important issues we choose to emphasize, the movements we encourage, and the projects we pursue. I sometimes wonder how we keep from flying apart, because our interests are rich, diverse, and even all over the board.

Now and again, we must pause amidst our restless pursuit of variety and remind ourselves that only one thing is important, namely, love. The traditional Christian doctrine of the Trinity may help us do this, if we let it. In this chapter we pause and we look at the convergence of our Christian historical, theological, and mystical sources of belief in the nature of God as three Persons who form one complete and unified entity whose love for one another overflows and embraces us as well. Is this not what we are all seeking in our own lives?

The Christian Scriptures reveal that God is the Almighty, absolutely Other from everything human, and Sovereign Lord above all the world. Yet the Christian God is not distant from us but involved in our human history and interested in our salvation, taking the initiative in pursuing our redemption. The Christian revelation presents God as merciful, impartial, and loving. Our God is an extraordinary combination of otherness and closeness, and this leads to our own faithful responses that combine reverence, praise, blessing, and obedience with peace, trust, love, and union.

We Christians believe Jesus Christ reveals the true nature of God as Father, a very personal kind of relationship, one that would not have been expected from a first century Jewish itinerant preacher. We believe he could do so only because he knew God intimately, so much so that we recognize him as the Son of God, the Word who existed from the very beginning with God, who was God. What an incredible claim: This human being was God-made-flesh, a person with two natures—divine and human—at the same time! And he told us that we, too, could be sons and daughters of God.

Jesus came to us in history as the agent of our redemption, and we recognize him as our Lord and Savior. His message is that our salvation consists of a relationship with God and not in blind obedience to a set of prescriptions. In fact, we believe Jesus is the very model of the kind of life God wants us to live, and our own holiness and fruitful fulfillment means modeling our lives on his. His revelation of the true nature of God challenges us to respond with action rather than words, with a mature faith rather than an immature adherence to doctrines and rules.

A mature Christian faith leads us to seek an efficacious union with Christ that is both personal and communal. It is transformational and redemptive for us all. But how do we accomplish this? We need help: an Advocate, perhaps, or a Counselor. Thus the revelation through Jesus that there is yet another face of the one God, a third "Person" equal to the Father and the Son, who is there to "fill the hearts of the faithful and kindle in them the fire of God's love."

This Holy Spirit unceasingly renews the Church throughout history, making Christ's message fresh and vital for all times and circumstances. This revelation teaches us that the Holy Spirit is the inner power in the life of each individual Christian: calling, unifying, and sanctifying each one, making each one into a new creation, and thereby satisfying each one's deepest yearnings for self-fulfillment. The Spirit also constitutes the new covenant community of the Church, uniting the baptized in love and freedom, and forming them into the Body of Christ. Finally, the Spirit creates a new revolution of service, extending Christ's plan for evangelization and love, and guiding the Church's ongoing mission and ministry.

So, in our search for meaning in life and for a deeper understanding of God, Christianity shows us that God is awesome but wishes us to be close. Then, our relationship to God should be modeled on that of Jesus. Moreover, we should not be overwhelmed either by the absolute otherness of God or by the power of God's intimate love for us, because the Holy Spirit is within us, responding through us to the divine reality. This is the mystery of the Christian God.

How can the Trinity be the model for our own journey? What is the relationship between faith and life? What can we discover from looking at the life of the three persons of God?

Some religions present an understanding of God which is quite apart and disconnected from the rules and regulations they use to direct the faithful in their daily lives. They do not base or model morality and discipleship on their image or understanding of God. Buddhism, Shinto, Hinduism, and most other religions are just a few examples of this approach.

Christianity's revelation begins with an experience of a human being, Jesus of Nazareth, and his teachings and way of life: "Everyone then who hears these words of mine and acts on them will be like a wise man who built his house upon rock" (Matthew 7:24). However, Jesus is not content to be a guru or wise man or prophet. He believes his life and teaching includes revealing the ways of the Father: "All things have been handed over to me by my Father; and no one knows the Son except the Father, and no one knows the Father except the Son and any one to whom the Son chooses to reveal him" (Matthew 11:27). In fact, in John's gospel Jesus tells Philip: "Whoever has seen me has seen the Father" (John 14:9).

Moreover, before his departure Jesus promises the presence of the Paraclete to continue his revelatory guidance. Christian followership, then, whether individual or communal, is based on the revealed portraits of Father, Son, and Holy Spirit, and calls adherents to model their lives on the qualities of God these portraits demand: "Be perfect, therefore, as your heavenly Father is perfect" (Matthew 5:48); "Learn from me, for I am gentle and humble in heart" (Matthew 11:29); "If we live by the Spirit, let us also be guided by the Spirit" (Galatians 5:25).

So the image of God on which we Christians base our lives is Trinitarian—three Persons in one God, whose relationship of love with one another constitute their very being for all eternity. Therefore, we believe one-sided representations of God or watered-down understandings of the Trinity produce inauthentic understandings, false societal structures, and unbalanced approaches to spirituality. This is pretty heavy stuff. It places a lot of pressure on us to live by something that even Saint Augustine said was impossible to understand completely! However, he and other saints of the Christian tradition have shown by word and example how the model of the Trinity can help us learn to love on our own spiritual journey, even if we do not understand its mystery.

The Trinity implies being constantly present to one another, the intimacy of immediacy, absolute reciprocity, and the centrality of community life. This emphasis on union and relatedness makes love the single great quality that unites us, as it does the Trinity. We are to be present to others and to the world in a transforming way that shows how love constitutes our very being.

If we have a Trinitarian understanding of love, for example, we don't get to pick and choose when we are going to love and when we are not. That is why Jesus couldn't fight back at his trial, why he insisted we had to turn the other cheek, why we have to love our sworn enemies, even if they don't love us back. Because the Trinity's love is eternal, it is always there, always on, always operative, always in play.

The Trinity constantly gives and receives fullness of life through eternity. That means it never started and will never stop giving and receiving love. It is who God is, what God does. Thus, unlike some other religions, we Christians believe that when we plug into divine life we are plugging into the fullness of love forever, even after our mortal lives have ended. Constantly drawing others into this fullness, God is lovingly involved in the growth of each and every one of us and of the entire human enterprise. That is why we Christians build our lives on genuine hope and see all growth in love as growth in the Lord.

So the Trinity is also the model and benchmark for our spiritual commitment: "The measure of people's love for God depends upon how deeply aware they are of God's love for them," said the fifth-century Christian, Saint Diadochus of Photice.

Complementing our scriptural and theological understanding of the revelation of the nature of God is our knowledge of salvation history, the basic elements of which are, perhaps, no better described than in the great liturgical hymn of the letter to the Ephesians (Ephesians 1:3-14). The hymn reminds us how God has abundantly blessed us and chosen us to attain our purpose in life, which is to stand before God in love as God's children. In this way, we find redemption and forgiveness.

The hymn proclaims the mystery of God's will, that everything be brought into union in Christ—the embodiment of love. Thus, we are redeemed as God's own chosen people, bound together in God's love, awestruck by the wisdom and power of God. We cannot but feel that our normal response should be worship and obedience to the all-powerful God. Yet God's revelation, clearly here in Ephesians but elsewhere too, says the desired response is: "Be holy and blameless before God in love" (Ephesians 1:4).

The Trinity stresses the relationships of love and the outreach in love to the world. It challenges us to seek a loving relationship with God and a loving communion among all people, whose purpose and destiny is to love, whether they are Christians or not.

God's purpose is love, God's gift is love, Jesus is the incarnation of love, and our response is love.

Scripture says that there is something that is growing within us, a seed of the divine life of love, struggling to come to fruition. The New Testament calls us "new creatures" and claims that as we struggle to discover our meaning and purpose in life, we realize that we come from a "new birth," a "birth from God." We are, it is shockingly proposed, a divine generation. What can this possibly mean?

In his one and only letter, Saint James, the "brother" of Jesus and the head of the early Church in Jerusalem, says that we are generated by the word of truth. He seems to be referring to the first creation in the book of Genesis, but now says this generation—and he does use the word *generate*—is created anew by means of the message of truth in the gospel: We are who we are because God has implanted a seed of divine life in us.

Saint Peter, the other acknowledged leader of the early Church, in his first letter links together the gift and call of love to this notion of us already having God's seed of life in us: "Now that you have purified your souls by your obedience to the truth so that you have genuine mutual love, love one another deeply from the heart. You have been born anew, not of perishable but of imperishable seed, through the living and enduring word of God" (1 Peter 1:22-23).

The realism of Peter's description is similar to that found in John's first letter: "Those who have been born of God do not sin, because God's seed abides in them; they cannot sin because they have been born of God" (1 John 3:9).

So we are born of God because the Creator has already given all human beings something of the divine life, a seed if you will. This gift of divine life blooms in us as we become conformed to the image of the Son, and we become children of God through the gift of the Holy Spirit. Thus, the triangle of relationships is complete. The consequence is that we must now allow ourselves to be led by the life of the Spirit within us. To be people of faith means to love God and to love all people—in other words, to become an intimate part of the divine dynamism of love.

Of course, we are constantly faced with the challenge "Why does God, the all-powerful Other, wish to be intimately present to us all?" This is the great Christian mystery: that God's entire strategy is one of love.

This vision of the ever-present, always available, eternally expanding love of God is often explored by Christian saints. Saint John of the Cross, a Spanish Carmelite mystic, presents us with perhaps the most beautiful expression of this vision, although he is one of many who take a similar approach.

John, who suffered much anxiety and doubt in his yearning for life with God, felt intense dissatisfaction with his search. As he comments on stanza six of his *Spiritual Canticle*: "Do not send me any more messengers. They cannot tell me what I must hear." John expresses his dissatisfaction at the mediated knowledge of God offered by others: "You have communicated by means of others, as if joking with me; now may you do so truly, communicating yourself by yourself" (*Canticle* 6, 6). Eventually, in his own mystical search, however, John catches glimpses of God's love that overwhelm him.

John discovered ways of encountering God that few others ever have, and he outlines two ways for us to search for God. One is the way of faith, presented in *The Ascent of Mount Carmel* and *The Dark Night of the Soul*. The other is the journey of love, presented in *The Spiritual Canticle* and *The Living Flame of Love*.

These books describe our spiritual journey to God. But John insists that the foundation of our spiritual journey is God's own journey to us, and he presents this part of his vision and understanding of God in a series of nine "romances." These beautiful poems portray the vision of the eternal life of God, the shared love in the intercommunication of the Trinity, their love-filled gift of creation, the incarnation, and Jesus' ministry of love. John presents the history of salvation as a project of love, overflowing from the Trinity's inner life of love. These nine romances, focusing as they do on God's plan for the world, complement the seeker's return journey to God for which the mystic saint is so much better known.

The nine interlinked romances start with the text from the Gospel of John, "In the beginning the Word was," and then present poetical and mystical reflections on the Trinity and the Incarnation. They are solidly based in the teachings of scripture, tradition, and theology, but they draw all these together with John of the Cross' additional spiritual depth and insight. The simple and beautifully expressed doctrines of these romances are rich in their biblical, Trinitarian, Christological, and ecclesiological understandings and vision, and they all center on love.

John's mystical vision of God's strategy of love begins with the inner life of God, which is one love that unites them. There are three persons, but "One love in them all makes them one Lover."

"For the three have one love," John writes. The three persons are together in constant unifying love. The Father then expresses how he loves the Son and how he could extend that love to others who are like the Son and love the Son. The Father offers the Son a bride (the created world) who will love him, and the Son says he will only choose a bride who "will burn with your (the Father's) love."

So the purpose of creation is to extend the love between Father and Son. The Father tells the Son to let creation begin, "For your love has deserved it," and the Son says he will give creation his love and lift up creation's love in return to the Father. The Son's love becomes so great that he is incarnated, "the lover becomes like the one loved," and in his new life he affirms his love is so strong "I will die for her" and "I will restore her to you."

So the cycle of love returns to the Trinity from which it started. John of the Cross confirms the essential conviction of God's own inner life of love and challenges us to live and spread that love.

We all search for fulfillment borne on by our restlessness for meaning and for God. We journey to become the best of which we are capable and find that in practice this means believing in the power of love. We seek a meaningful life based on faith-filled experiences of a love that guides our search. In fact, it is the experience of love that gives our lives meaning: love that at times presents intuitions into a greater love beyond normal horizons. Wherever we turn, we hear the call of love.

In turning to what little we know of the God whom we seek, we find our Christian traditions present us with an awesome God who longs to be close to us. Our belief and faith is in the God who is Trinity, a communion of love who becomes the model for all aspects of our lives. Our God of love calls for a response of love, and this response is in many ways natural to us because God has placed a seed of the divine life of love in each of us.

Our own searching and yearning for fulfillment, whatever forms they take, find answers in love. Our tradition, revelation, faith, and mystical reflection all point in the direction of love being the answer to our longings. Our hearts are restless until they rest in love, Saint

Augustine might have said.

When we look at our God, our questioning of creation, our purpose in life, we find answers in the fact that all these are part of God's strategy of love. God's love is benevolent, and God apparently takes pleasure in this love for us. We discover how gratifying God's love is and then discover the benevolent nature of God—a love beyond all normal horizons. This is a wonderful revelation for those whose hearts are large enough for it.

We must all revise our idea of what it means to be a Christian. We have always given at least lip service and sometimes more to the importance of love, but it is hardly the central issue of our contemporary life of faith. Yet we need to be clear: "The aim of...instruction is love that comes from a pure heart, a good conscience, and sincere faith" (1 Timothy 1:5).

In speaking to his Father, Jesus says "And this is eternal life, that they may know you, the only true God, and Jesus Christ whom you have sent" (John 17:3). Elsewhere, speaking of this eternal life we seek, Jesus explains that it means appreciating that the Father loves the Son, the Son loves humanity, and humanity is called to live on in this divine love.

Jesus tells us that we prove this love by keeping his commandments, but the commandments are means to love not ends in themselves: "Just as I have loved you, you should love one another. By this everyone will know that you are my disciples, if you have love for one another" (John 13:34-35).

This love opens us to something beyond comprehension: "The Father himself loves you, because you have loved me and have believed that I came from God" (John 16:27). Jesus' conclusion is simple. "As the Father has loved me, so I have loved you; abide in my love" (John 15:9). The relationship of Father and Son becomes the model for our own love for God and one another: "Those who love me will keep my word, and my Father will love them, and we will come to them and make our home with them" (John 14:23).

QUESTIONS FOR DISCUSSION
FOR PERSONAL REFLECTION ··

1. *What are three signs of love you see in the world? Where do they come from? How do they exhibit "the intimacy of immediacy, absolute reciprocity, and the centrality of community life"?*

2. *How do you personally fit into God's strategy of love? Who are your human role models for how to love? Name them. Does the Trinity provide a role model for your efforts to love? If so, how? Be specific.*

3. *"All you need is love," sang the Beatles. Is that true? Why or why not? How can you begin to live differently with a new understanding of your life in God and God's life in you?*

Love's Pain

A WORLD CRYING FOR LOVE

As God sees the world tottering to ruin because of fear, he acts unceasingly to bring it back by love, invite it by grace, to hold it by charity and clasp it firmly with affection.

Peter Chrysologus, *Sermon* 147

All or nothing he accepts....

God does not bother with half-hearted love.

Richard Rolle, *The Fire of Love*, chapter 23

Because of his tender love for all those who are to be saved our good Lord comforts us at once and sweetly, as if to say, "It is true that sin is the cause of all this pain; but it is all going to be alright; it is all going to be alright; everything is going to be alright." These words were said most tenderly, with never a hint of blame either to me or to any of those to be saved.

Julian of Norwich, *Revelations of Divine Love*, chapter 27

Many waters cannot quench love,
neither can floods drown it.
If a man offered for love all the wealth of his house
it would be utterly scorned.

Song of Songs, 8:7

FOCUS FOR THIS CHAPTER

*The world in which we live
is a world largely without love,
and it is our job to show
how the way of love can work.*

- *Examine the lack of love in our world and its causes.*

- *Identify the violence, untruthfulness, fear, hate, and meaninglessness we experience in our own lives.*

- *Admit the reduced ideals of Christian love that creep into our daily lives.*

- *Seek deliverance from spiritual mediocrity and regain our vocation to spread the way of love.*

- *Recognize our own unloving attitudes and learn how to change them.*

A colleague recently wrote a book on the need for a spirit of forgiveness in contemporary leaders. My friend writes beautifully, with a lyrical and poetical language that is haunting. However, the subject matter was frightening, as he detailed the horrors and violence against opponents and innocents that have characterized the hate-filled reactions of many so-called "leaders" (many of them self-described Christians) just in the last century or so.

Among the many stories he narrated were the Rwandan genocide; the murder of innocent men, women, and children, and the complete destruction of the town of Lidice, near Prague, by the Nazis; the rape of 20,000 women during the Serbo-Croatian conflict in the name of ethnic cleansing; and the Big Hole massacre in which U.S. military murdered men, women, and children of the Nez Perce.

In each of these stories he describes how leadership failed when it was filled with hatred instead of forgiveness. He could find only a few significant leaders who exemplified the forgiveness he sought— Mother Teresa, President Cory Aquino, Archbishop Desmond Tutu, and a few others.

Striving to implement God's project of love is an uphill battle. We must admit it seems there is an organized opposition to love that has taken over our contemporary world, and the way of love mostly seems a naïve and unattainable dream to most people. We are not always—or even usually—surrounded by love in our communities or our Christian churches. Rather, we often face violence, untruthfulness, fear, hate, a sense of the ultimate meaninglessness of life. People—including ourselves and our loved ones—seem to make unloving decisions. Humanity has created its own hell on earth by driving love out of our lives.

Ours is a fearful world, whether it is fear of our self-destruction in war or environmental degradation or fear of our materialistic approach that puts things and organizations before people or fear that we could descend into some "Lord of the Flies" type of society. We are oppressed by fear of abuse in its many forms. We recoil from suffering and death. We are terrified by the unknown.

The fear we experience is understandable because we live in a world where violence is tolerated and viewed as an acceptable way of responding to conflicting values. Nations that increase their arsenals of weapons become afraid of other countries that do the same. We human beings find new ways of killing one another on a scale beyond all previous experience. Terrorism, torture, and the use of rape, hunger, and thirst to wage war is now accepted. Drones do our killing for us, at no risk to "our" soldiers or civilians.

Evil politicians deliberately use genocide and ethnic cleansing and social displacement as policy. We have seen a few individuals whose greed for wealth and power has completely ruined stable economies in a matter of a few years, including in our own country. People called to serve others in positions of leadership, even religious leaders, have concentrated on controlling other people's lives. The prophet's words are so true. "O my people, your leaders mislead you, and confuse the course of your paths" (Isaiah 3:12). The world is full of leaders without love.

And individuals all over the world accept this culture of violence. They set up gangs to maintain it, establishing lifestyles in which racism, sexism, and homophobia are not only accepted but celebrated. Mafia-style groups and drug cartels are growing in many countries, spreading their oppression and violence all over the world. People are paid to be violent in order to deliberately foster division and to ensure the breakdown of society. Some make their living by hacking into computers to destroy other people's lives or property; others make money by stealing the identities of innocent people; and still others pirate the work of others for easy gain.

All of us participate in this violence of our world. We keep politicians in power, we tolerate religious absolutism, we support corrupt businesses, we join in the destruction of our environment, we vote single-issue politics, and we cannot be bothered with opposing violence as long as it is far away and affects people we don't know. We allow our economy to favor the rich and punish the poor. Many resolve relationship problems with domestic violence, including abuse of spouses, the elderly, and the young. There are also many forms of violence to ourselves in the form of abuse of drugs, alcohol, and sex, and also in lifestyles of too much work or too little work.

We also live in a world that fears truth. The psalmist seems to be describing our contemporary society when he says, "You love evil more than good, and lying more than speaking the truth" (Psalm 52:3).

Jesus was known for his truthfulness: "Teacher, we know that what you say and teach is correct, and you show no partiality but teach the way of God in accordance with the truth" (Luke 20:21). But do we speak and insist on the truth?

Many of our so-called leaders live lies. They withhold truth, give half-truths, hire lawyers to lie for them, take the Fifth Amendment, apologize without ever admitting they did anything wrong, and so on. They are trained to avoid the truth, will not answer a straightforward question, and hire spin doctors to slant their lies. We have reached a point where we no longer expect the truth from large segments of society, and especially from our leaders. As the prophet Isaiah warned: "Justice is turned back, and righteousness stands at a distance; for truth stumbles in the public square, and uprightness cannot enter" (Isaiah 59:14).

Many religious leaders—and their followers—have been caught up in this movement away from truth telling. We Christians have had our own cases of lying and cover-ups. Religions' half truths frequently come in the neglect of teachings that those in power find inconvenient. For example, in the Catholic Church many aspects of Vatican II, including the roles of women, freedom of conscience, and charisms of the faithful, are ignored if not denied.

Imposing the narrow views of one in-group while other positions are clearly and equally acceptable is another distortion of truth. Imposing a particular position while knowing others to be acceptable is untruthful and unethical. Many religious leaders give the impression they actually believe that every personal opinion of theirs must be the truth for everyone else. Hypocrisy has become a characteristic of contemporary religious leadership, linked to increased careerism and often exaggerated wealth accumulation.

This is all so different than what the prophets promised: "The effect of righteousness will be peace, and the result of righteousness, quietness and trust forever" (Isaiah 32:17). Is our world so bad simply because we human beings are lacking in the righteousness of love? It would seem so.

We violate the true order even in our relating to God. We become self-destructive in excluding spirituality from our lives, in giving inadequate attention to our own best spiritual interests, in justifying our spiritual isolation because of the failures of others, in stunting our spiritual growth through deliberate ignorance of the life of God. When violence, fear, and lying become part of the very fabric of everyday life, we can expect a proportional loss of our appreciation of God: "And because of the increase of lawlessness, the love of many will grow cold" (Matthew 24:12).

Living in a world of non-love is not something we merely grow to accept. No! It is a way of life we deliberately cultivate. We allow and at times support and enjoy the polarization and bigotry that contemporary political movements engender. Our national elections are largely won on the basis of negative campaigning, and of course we get the politicians this process produces. We listen to endless commercials, interviews, discussions, and party positions that consist in nothing but cultivated distortion, deliberate misrepresentation, and mutual hate. Nowadays there are endless numbers of operatives, both hired and freelance, who make their living on hate-filled books, talk-shows, blogs, and films. The purpose of these presentations is pure rabble rousing—and we are the rabble! No persuasion of opinion is needed or even sought; periodicals, TV programs, radio shows, and Internet sites are directed solely to fanatics who already agree to further arouse their fanaticism, and many of us ordinary people get caught up in it too.

Labeling others in ways that encourage people to despise them is now a feature of contemporary life. Labeling as a means of alienating, attacking, and destroying is also part of the struggle among religions, and between traditions within a religion, and among various theological positions within each group. And if there is no one else to attack, the religious attack the atheists and the atheists attack the believers.

Jesus, on the other hand, says: "I came that they may have life and have it abundantly" (John 10:10). At times we Christians act as if we never heard this. We adapt the ways of the prevailing culture rather than offer what Paul calls "a still more excellent way" (1 Corinthians 12:31). He then breaks into his ode to love:

> Love is patient; love is kind; love is not envious or boastful or arrogant or rude. It does not insist on its own way; it is not irritable or resentful; it does not rejoice in wrongdoing, but rejoices in the truth.

> 1 Corinthians 13:4-6

This is what we Christians have to offer the world: a more excellent way, the way of love. We don't have anything else—or anything better—to bring to this tired world. Often we Christians act as if convinced our own lives have no meaning. While God has placed gifts of personality in each of us, we stagnate; our values never come together in a clear approach to life. We do not seem capable of integrating our philosophy of life into a major commitment of our life values.

How many of us give no impression of understanding our purpose in life, our mission, our destiny. Yet each of us has a personal calling, a destiny that is the result of the Trinity's initiative of love. Love does not show itself in apathy and helplessness. Even though we may feel powerless in the face of the multitude of problems in the world, each one of us is filled with the great realities of God's love, called to be more, to love more, and to serve more. What happens to us in this challenge? We must live the love and the truth that reflects God's life within us, no matter what the cost. Anything less is meaningless.

The Church's Morning Prayer sums up the feelings that must be ours: "The love that we have wasted, O God of love, renew" (Hymn week, 3, Tuesday). Our world is filled with damaged people: people who could love but hate, who could dialogue but divide, who could care but despise, who could unify but polarize. They need redemption from their lack of love, and we can bring it to them.

In dealing with sin we often try to cure the symptoms but not the cause. Until this world of ours turns to love, however, we humans will always wallow in the superficiality of our unloving attitudes. Some say the way of love is too naïve and can never work. What they fail to admit is that the way of non-love has never worked. We need to demonstrate by our lives that love does work. Even if it is not the "way of the world."

At times we act towards others as if their lives have no value or meaning. Many governments, businesses, and individuals waste the earth and its resources for power and financial gain. People starve to death, others die socially because of a lack of education, and others are ostracized by an arrogant elite. Every nation has its untouchables, its lepers, its social and religious outcasts. Modern-day Pharisees lock people out of the advantages of society, establish laws that take advantage of the poor, ignore justice in the name of social and religious appearances, and push a cult of personality. They have built a world that will crush us.

We must act to change direction and avoid the catastrophe of creating a hell on earth in which people have forgotten how to love. Yet our spiritual lives have too little emphasis on the goal and strategy of love.

All sin is a lack of love and manifests itself in the three fundamental focuses of life. All sin stems from a lack of love for oneself, for others in just and loving relationships, and for others in organized community. These three focuses of life give birth to the three great energies of the soul, three qualities that are so central to the gospel they are called the "evangelical counsels." Here they are:

- *The spirit of poverty directs good relationships within ourselves, making sure that we become our true selves and not some artificial self that is based on an accumulation of "things."*
- *The spirit of chastity directs us to a just relationship to people, never using them for our own satisfaction but treating them with loving respect.*

- *The spirit of obedience directs us to listen to the voice of community, recognizing in community development the intimate plan of God (obedience comes from a Latin word, obaudire, meaning "to listen intently").*

Some decisions are unloving to ourselves. Continuing to live in a world of non-love without doing anything about the violence, untruthfulness, fear, hate, and meaninglessness of life is a fundamentally unloving choice. Sin is a lack of love for our own authenticity: our open and secret sins preventing each of us from being the best person we can be. Likewise, the lack of response to the grace of God thwarts our individual potential for spiritual growth.

This deliberate lack of investment in our own growth is also seen in an unwillingness to develop anything other than superficial relationships in which we never tap the depth of commitment that is latent within us. Some decisions are unloving to others in interpersonal relationships. In the worst form this includes using people in slave labor, child labor, prostitution, abuse of the young, the elderly, and women; and of course benefiting from any of these in the products we buy. It also includes affairs, relationships of convenience, and any way in which we deliberately use someone else for our own temporary gain. Deliberately using one's authority over others to inflict harm or to obtain gain is sinful: torture, disdain, sexual favors, punishment, abuse, put down, or control. Depriving people of their livelihood is a deliberate lack of love, especially if those in power receive exorbitant salaries at the expense of other people. Accepting position and salary which one knows to be only possible by depriving others of what is just is unacceptable. One of the difficulties of interpersonal development is that we get to know other people's sensitivities and can then hurt them where and how it is particularly painful. Unloving is at its worst when based on former love.

Then some decisions are unloving when they are based within the neglect of community. The worst forms of community violation are in human trafficking in sex, drugs, or illegal immigration. Others would include the deliberate isolating of ourselves from community development and its struggles for growth, whether in political, social, or church life. A lack of dialogue and a total disdain of other people's opinions, ignoring people's rights of participation in organizations—whether in civil or ecclesiastical life—are all forms of deliberate unloving behavior. Abuse of political processes and a lack of respect for others' role in community are also forms of non-love.

Unloving decisions destroy us from within. No matter how unloving people become, however, all retain a faint remembrance of the divine life of love meant for them. This love will never die, for God will always love us. "O give thanks to the Lord, for he is good; his steadfast love endures forever!" (Psalm 118:1).

QUESTIONS FOR DISCUSSION
FOR PERSONAL REFLECTION ·····································

1. *Just how far is the world away from operating by the way of love? Give examples and explain why you think this is the case. What can be done about it?*

2. *Name the major areas in your personal and professional life that need healing and transformation by love. What could you do in the next month to make it happen? What is blocking you from trying?*

3. *How does lack of focus on yourself cause you to make unloving decisions? How about lack of focus on others in personal relationships? How about lack of focus on others in the community? Explore how you might regain your focus in all three areas.*

Love's Hope

OUR VOCATION TO LOVE

For God is not known by argument, but by what we do and how we love.

Richard Rolle, *The Fire of Love*, Prologue

Take, O Lord, and receive all my liberty, my memory, my understanding, and my entire will, all that I have and possess. Thou hast given it all to me, to Thee O Lord, I return it. All is Thine; dispose of it according to Thy will. Give me Thy love and Thy grace, for this is enough for me.

Ignatius of Loyola, *Fourth Week of the Exercises*

Therefore I will leave on one side everything I can think, and choose for my love that thing which I cannot think! Why? Because he may well be loved, but not thought. By love he can be caught and held, but by thinking never.

Cloud of Unknowing, #6

"But how, then, am I to love God?" You must love Him as if He were a Non-God, a Non-Spirit, a Non-Person, a Non-Substance: love him simply as the One, the pure and absolute Unity in which is no trace of duality. And into this One, we must let ourselves fall continually from being into non-being. God helps us to do this.

Dag Hammarskjold, *Markings*, "The Night is Neigh"

FOCUS FOR THIS CHAPTER ··

God calls us to make choices that are always based on love.

- *Deepen our understanding of the intertwined and indivisible relationship between faith and love.*

- *Reflect on the choice between loving and following rules.*

- *Explore a spiritual asceticism based on love.*

- *Examine our own lives of love alongside the four ways Jesus taught us to love.*

- *Let the Trinity draw us to our vocation to bring new levels of love to the world.*

I have had opportunities to meet several extraordinary people whose entire lives were dedicated in love to others. I met Mother Teresa of Calcutta and heard her describe what she saw as the purpose of her life. It was an extraordinary encounter.

I taught a course on the Gospel of Luke to Jean Vanier and the English-speaking leaders of L'Arche communities and felt blessed to interact with Jean Vanier every day of the course and appreciate the total dedication of his life in the service of others.

I also had the special opportunity to meet and listen to Carlo Caretto, the disciple and presenter of the insights of Brother Charles de Foucauld. It was shocking to learn how de Foucauld had abandoned everything to live in a loving obscurity.

These three—a simple but powerful nun who gave herself to the abandoned poor; a son of the Governor General of Canada who left all and gave himself to serve the disabled; and a leader of Italian Catholic Action who left politics and organizational leadership to become a Little Brother known only for love—these, and others too, have left an indelible mark on me, as people who desire only to live for love.

Jesus has called those of us who are his followers to become a community dedicated to love. In spite of humanity's many failures, love is a living reality in our present world. If we believe this with all our being and hand over our entire existence to God's love, we can become participants in the greatest project of human existence: helping to bring about the "kingdom" or "reign" of transforming love "on earth as it is in heaven," as Jesus taught us to pray.

Our faith can never be merely a mental acknowledgement of the truth that Jesus is our savior; it must also include the practical acceptance of Jesus as God's gift of love to us, as the embodiment of God's love, as the teacher of God's love, and as the one who calls us to the way of God's love.

By this love he saves us. Only when our faith includes intimacy with the God of love can it be genuine. That is why the psalmist tells us that love and truth go together in God: "I will sing of your steadfast love, O Lord, forever; with my mouth I will proclaim your faithfulness to all generations. I declare that your steadfast love is established forever; your faithfulness is as firm as the heavens" (Psalm 89:1-2).

Our response to God's invitation to love is made real in our faith in Jesus, who is "the pioneer and perfecter of our faith" (Hebrews 12:2). Our baptismal vocation challenges us to give ourselves in absolute allegiance to Christ, to become a new creation in him, and to accept a new mode of living based on love. God calls us to the perfection of faith, hope, and love, each being a grace lovingly bestowed on us in Jesus.

But faith is not an abstract, intellectual assent but always includes love. It is not so much that faith is our acknowledgment of God bu rather it is God'c acknowledgment of us, and we reply with loving gratitude. So our Christian faith should not produce so much a belief system as a life of love. In other words, we do not believe and therefore love God; rather, we feel loved by God and love God and our fellow humans in return, and therefore we believe because of that experience.

Saint Paul's letters, the Synoptic Gospels, and especially the Gospel of John and his letters, link faith inextricably to love. Christian life is not regulated by detailed laws but by the two fundamental attitudes of faith and love, which on reflection become one single orientation of life—to live faith in love. Jesus is the revealer of love, and if we wish to be people of faith we must be enthused with this awareness, understand it, apply it, and live it in practice.

Paul sums up this attitude of every disciple: "May I never boast of anything except the cross of our Lord Jesus Christ, by which the world has been crucified to me and I to the world" (Galatians 6:14). The cross is the proof of the depth of Jesus' love and a reminder to each of us of the very real cost of the way of love. Our dedication in faith to the way of love is a conversion away from self to others and to God, and it becomes our experience of being baptized in Christ's death.

As we move away from our natural self-centeredness to focus on the love of others and of God, we are moving from death to life; from the non-love that is sin to being truly alive to others and to God. In this way our faith grows into love: "For while we live, we are always being given up to death for Jesus' sake, so that the life of Jesus may be made visible in our mortal flesh" (2 Corinthians 4:10-12). This is part of the severe reality of following the way of love; it is also every disciple's mature response to faith.

We feel called to reject this world's reign of selfishness, greed, and self-satisfaction and to accept the new kingdom of God's selfless love. This is a first step towards the maturity of Christian love and implies the reversal of all the values towards love espoused by the kingdom of darkness. The way is clear and straightforward: "Love your enemies, do good to those who hate you, bless those who curse you, pray for those who abuse you.... Do to others as you would have them do to you" (Luke 6:27-28, 31).

This is the Christian mindset that gives us such peace and joy. It starts with the struggle against our indifference to others and to God, and it ends with our total commitment to love. What could be better or more exciting than that?

We Christians acknowledge that we live in a disordered world that has lost the essential values of love. We know we can be as self-absorbed, consumed by possessions, and motivated by money as those without any faith. As we seek to make decisions that subordinate ourselves to the life of the Spirit and to the way of love, we often regress instead of making progress. We fail to follow the way, even though we would like to, and we do not know why.

So our first task, even preliminary to the journey, is to purify any love that is not of God. Love cannot be diversified in many objects, it must be total, unified, and integrated: "You shall love the Lord your God with all your heart, and with all your soul, and with all your mind" (Matthew 22:37).

Our pursuit of Christian love is based on our doing the most loving thing in any given circumstance. We bear the seed of God's love within us, but must make this alive in daily choices that result from discernment and perseverance. It is a journey that consists in total honesty with our vision of love, always choosing the most loving thing to do: "For the Son of God, Jesus Christ, whom we proclaimed among you, was not 'Yes and No,' but in him it is always 'Yes'" (2 Corinthians 1:19).

Making choice-oriented love decisions is a form of discernment. It is difficult but particularly necessary when the conditions of our world are so contrary to justice and love that, at times, it seems scarcely possible to make genuinely Christian decisions at all. We cannot just wait for good and loving things to happen; we must make decisions that produce such situations. We can follow any of the usual methods of discernment: evaluate the pros and cons of each possible decision, reflect on the consequences of each advantage and disadvantage, ask for the guidance of the Holy Spirit, and then make the decision in peace.

Of course we cannot come directly to discernment without being dedicated to the preparations needed to train ourselves to perceive God's love in the world, which is everywhere but sometimes hidden. This implies the usual practices of self-control, ethical behavior, prayer, knowledge of Jesus' teachings, and dedication to the community of faith. Making decisions can be reactive to situations that arise or it can be proactive in effort to change the values of our world. These decisions do not just involve our personal lives but need to include social, church, and political situations in contemporary life. They are decisions that involve risks.

We manifest our decisions based on love through our bodies much more than our minds. We are not pure spiritual beings like angels but physical, fleshy, mortal ones who express the deepest values of our inner spirit through our bodies. For us, our bodies are the expression of our souls. Showing another person our trust, understanding, compassion, or sense of communion—all require real physicality. Working to change contemporary injustices, to confront unacceptable cultural values, to challenge the lovelessness of society—all require presence, effort, and role-modeling. Being sensitive to the aspirations of the poor and disinherited, comforting the unhappy, the neglected, and the abused, responding to the hopes for liberty, for friendship, and for family well-being—all require genuine involvement.

Jesus refers to two great commandments: love of God and love of neighbor. Regarding the second commandment he insists, "You shall love your neighbor as yourself" (Matthew 22:39). This teaching on loving others as we love ourselves is repeated seven times in the New Testament, and Saint James calls it "the royal law" (James 2:8). It is not unlike Jesus' statement in the Gospel of Luke, "Do to others as you would have them do to you" (Luke 6:31).

While loving others as we love ourselves is a noble goal, Jesus seeks more than this as a measure of one's commitment to the way of love. In fact, there are four progressive statements made by Jesus; the first three are commandments and the fourth is in the form of a prayer for the quality of love his disciples should show:

- *Love others as you love yourself.*
- *Love others as you wish to love Jesus.*
- *Love others as Jesus loves you.*
- *Love others as Jesus and the Father love each other.*

These four stages of love form the ascetical program for those who wish to follow the way of love. By *ascetical* I mean the disciplined, ongoing, sometimes difficult pursuit of holiness, from the Greek word for "training" or "exercise." I am not proposing that we all head to the monasteries! What I am suggesting is that if we want to follow the way of love, we have to be serious about it, even though most of us will do so for the most part in the midst of our ordinary daily lives on our jobs, in our relationships, and through our civic and community involvement.

Paul was convinced that every other commandment was summed up in this one on loving your neighbor as *yourself*: "The commandments...are summed up in this word. 'Love your neighbor as yourself.' Love does no wrong to a neighbor; therefore, love is the fulfilling of the law" (Romans 13:9).

Certainly this is the beginning of mature love, when we move away from loving others simply because we need them and dedicate ourselves to love others because we simply recognize them as loveable. Of course, this way to love depends on our own healthy and mature self-love, self-acceptance, and self-affirmation. We can hardly love others healthily and maturely unless we can love ourselves that way. The capacity to genuinely love ourselves is part of the world vision that leads to the way of love for others.

Thinking about how we love ourselves, we quickly appreciate that we believe we are loveable; have value in ourselves and not because of our possessions or position; lose nothing by comparison with others; consider we are trustworthy, sincere, and valuable to others. We also think we are worthy of others' love, support, and friendship; that they should respect our good name; that they ought to speak well of us, include us in their discussions, listen to our opinions, and so on. It is easy to list how we think others should love us.

This, then, is how we should love others. Loving others as we love ourselves is also the practical challenge to human rights; we expect ours to be respected, and the way of love includes the multi-layered struggle for the rights of others.

The second degree of love is to love others as we would like to love Jesus were we to encounter him. In the final judgment scene in Matthew's gospel, Jesus speaks about his disciples' treatment of the hungry, thirsty, naked, sick, imprisoned, and anyone who is a stranger. He concludes, "Truly I tell you, just as you did it to one of the least of these who are members of my family, you did it to me" (Matthew 25:40).

Manifesting faith in the way of love implies this attitude of loving others as we would love Jesus. It requires meditation on the life of Jesus, like Mary, the sister of Lazarus. She symbolizes for us the attentive contemplation on the life and values of Jesus that allows us to discern what Jesus would do in a particular situation (John 11:32-33).

We also see many examples in the gospels of what Jesus would like our attitudes toward others to be. Moreover, Jesus insists that no one can legislate love. We must base our responses on an inner spirit that impels us to always give priority to others, not on some rule that tells us what to do or not to do in every situation.

In the fifth chapter of the Gospel of Matthew, right after the Beatitudes, Jesus gives six examples of contrasting legalistic approaches to others with inner transforming love. He shows us how difficult it is to love him in others, a section that culminates with the ultimate challenge to universal love: "Be perfect, therefore, as your heavenly Father is perfect" (Matthew 5:48).

This rebirth to loving everyone as we would love Jesus is possible because of the Father's guidance. "If God were your Father, you would love me" (John 8:42), a mandate lived out with everyone we meet. The follower of the way looks to others with the enthusiasm of loving Christ: "Who will separate us from the love of Christ? Will hardships, or distress, or persecution, or famine, or nakedness, or peril, or sword?… No, in all these things we are more than conquerors through him who loved us" (Romans 8:35, 37). When this understanding dawns on us that we must love everyone in the way we would want to love Jesus, then we begin to hand ourselves over to the Lord whom we love.

The third level of love is to love others as Jesus loves us: "He who says he abides in him ought to walk in the same way in which he walked" (1 John 2:6).

During the Last Supper before his anticipated death, Jesus solemnly speaks to his disciples and gives them and us this third degree of love: "I give you a new commandment, that you love one another. Just as I have loved you, you also should love one another" (John 13:34). This seems an impossible challenge, and yet Jesus presents it to us as a command while at the same time saying it is a gift to us.

Jesus came into this loveless world, filled with the enduring love of the Father, brought to the world and to each of us the transforming love of God, and gave his life for love of us. When he washed his disciples' feet, Jesus gave them a standard by which to judge their love: "I have set you an example, that you also should do as I have done" (John 13:15). And after explaining to the disciples that he is the Good Shepherd whose love is such that he lays down his life for his sheep, Jesus says, "for this reason the Father loves me, because I lay down my life in order to take it up again" (John 10:17).

This is the level of love we are to strive to imitate. The gift and command of selfless love for others in imitation of Jesus comes in a section of the gospel when Jesus also says: "Very truly, I tell you, the one who believes in me will also do the works that I do and, in fact, will do greater works that these" (John 14:12). Jesus' command that we love others as he loves us is complemented with his assurances that he will answer our prayers so that the entire and ongoing project of love he begins can be brought to completion. As disciples, we pray that Jesus will help us do the greater works of selfless love of others. If we are faithful to this vision of loving others as Jesus loved us, then nothing can impede such heroic Christian lives as ours.

In practice this challenge means "bearing with one another in love" (Ephesians 4:2), that is, welcoming everyone we encounter in life, offering limitless forgiveness to others, loving everyone as members of our own family, being like the Father in the story of the prodigal son, and being filled with compassion for others in their failures.

Of course, to love as Jesus loved requires that we remain in union with him as branches on the vine, having always the same mind and attitudes as the Christ, never losing sight of the Jesus who leads us in our faith, so that eventually we can say with Paul: "It is no longer I who live, but it is Christ who lives in me" (Galatians 2:20).

The fourth, final, and greatest expression of love comes during the great prayer of Jesus toward the end of the Last Supper. He says, "Holy Father, protect them in your name that you have given me, so that they may be one, as we are one" (John 17:11). He continues to pray, "so that they may be one, as we are one, I in them and you in me, that they may become completely one, so that the world may know that you have sent me and have loved them even as you have loved me" (John 17:23).

With this prayer we disciples are sent into the world, consecrated in truth, and entrusted with the mission of bringing love to the world. For our success Jesus re-offers himself in sacrifice, as he will lay down his life for us, his friends. Jesus anticipates the success of our mission and claims that the unity and love we spread throughout the world and over the centuries will be proof of his redemptive mission to the world. This unity is not something that happens at the end of the world but is a present reality that is so evident it calls others to think beyond their normal horizons about the love of God.

So the unity of the Father and the Son is repeated in the community of love between Jesus and us, his disciples. This love is inconceivable without Jesus' help, and he assures the disciples he will send the Paraclete to support them in their efforts. So once again, love is a labor of all three members of the Trinity, and we are invited into it. But ours is a love that provokes the world to judgment: "By this everyone will know that you are my disciples, if you have love for one another" (John 13:35).

That's a pretty heavy criterion. Not much wiggle room. As Christians, we are called to share in the awesome transcendent reality of the Trinity's love for one another; a love that is their essence. Likewise, we cease to be Christian the minute we cease to love, although repentance and forgiveness are always but a metanoia away.

Christian love is our vocation. We have but to accept it and follow the way laid out for us by Jesus himself.

QUESTIONS FOR DISCUSSION
FOR PERSONAL REFLECTION ···

1. *Name three people you have met or learned about who lived a vocation of Christian love. What is it about the way they love that strikes you? What prevents you from loving as they do? What could you do about that?*

2. *What does "a spiritual asceticism based on love" mean to you? How do you make your spiritual choices and decisions now? How might they change if you made all of them based on love? Be specific as to what would be different and why.*

3. *Which of the four "ways" to judge your love (love others as you love yourself, love others as you love Jesus, love others as Jesus loves us, love others as the Trinity loves one another and us) do you use? Give examples. What would it take for you to try some of the other ways?*

Love's Vision

SHARING LOVE IN COMMUNITY

Love one another, all of you, with a heart above all divisions.

Ignatius of Antioch, *Letter to the Trallians*

The day will come when, after harnessing space, the winds, the tides, and gravitation, we shall harness for God the energies of love. And, on that day, for the second time in the history of the world, we shall have discovered fire.

Teilhard de Chardin, *Toward the Future*

A day comes when the soul belongs to God, when it not only consents to love but when truly and effectively it loves. Then in its turn it must cross the universe to go to God. The soul does not love like a creature with created love. The love within it is divine, uncreated; for it is the love of God for God which is passing through it. God alone is capable of loving God. We can only consent to give up our own feelings so as to allow free passage in our soul for this love. That is the meaning of denying oneself. We are created for this consent, and for this alone.

Simone Weil, *The Love of God and Affliction*
(communication sent to Fr. Perrin)

*To those who are called,
beloved of God the Father and kept for Jesus Christ:
May mercy, peace, and love be multiplied....
Keep yourselves in the love of God.*

Jude, 1-2, 21

FOCUS FOR THIS CHAPTER ···

> *We are God's communities of faith and love,*
> *living in reconciling love and*
> *sharing our faith-filled love with others.*

- *Remind ourselves that building up community at all levels of our lives is an essential element of the Christian strategy toward the world.*

- *Re-examine community, incarnation, and service as the three vehicles for the transforming power of love.*

- *Explore whether or not reconciliation is a normal characteristic of our attitude to others.*

- *Recognize how community must begin at the local level and then "percolate" into higher and larger levels of the world and the Church.*

- *Consider how we can be more prudent and effective in bringing love to our contemporary world.*

*T*he purpose of creation is the expansion of love—that the love of God for God passes through us and returns to God. This is love's vision, and our part in this vision is to build loving communities at all levels of our life.

I have heard from many people who attended the Second Vatican Council that the greatest insight of the Council—the one that changed the way the participants viewed everything else—was the change in the Church's awareness of itself as a community rather than as an institution. In fact, the Council lasted four years, and a study of the editing of its documents evidences a three-fold change in four years, a genuine conversion. Yet surely, the Council was not some great study session—even though it did produce two thirds of all council documents in the history of the Church. (Think about that!)

Rather, Vatican II was a spiritual experience that we have to believe was guided by the Holy Spirit. Its revelation of self came in three stages. First, the Church became aware of itself as a community of believers. Second, it realized it was a community of believers that existed in the very heart of the world God loves. Third, it became convinced it was a community of believers inserted into the world God loves to serve all others. Community, incarnation, and service—the three great awarenesses of the Church in Council, are the vehicle for the transforming power of love.

Early Christians clearly understood that authentic conversion included the acceptance of a community dimension to their new life. This emphasis on community today is not meant to be a denial of or stand in opposition to our spiritual development as individuals, but it does indicate our conviction that to be dedicated to community is the finest way to affirm and live out the best in ourselves.

Throughout Jesus' ministry he always gave his attention to his group of followers. They were his companions, his community, his family: "He called to him those whom he wanted, and they came to him" (Mark 3:13). We rarely see Jesus alone in Scripture, except for his temptations in the desert before he began his ministry, and while he called individuals to follow him, that implied joining his community as well.

From the early days, and especially after the Ascension and Pentecost, the followers of Jesus became profoundly aware that they were a special group. When others accepted the Lord's call, they were "added" to the group. We read, "And day by day the Lord added to their number those who were being saved" (Acts 2:47). So part of the proclamation of the early disciples was a call to membership in their community. It was part and parcel of their understanding of their mission.

So unless we Christians exist as a community, we do not exist as an authentic manifestation of Jesus' followers to the world. Community is the way of life to which God calls us, and it focuses us on what Jesus hopes will become the revelatory ultimate value: love. The vision Jesus offers us is one of universal unity—a life of union that prepares us for union with God. The basic communion with Jesus that constitutes Christian renewal gives rise to the communion of us Christians among ourselves and eventually with all humanity and all creation.

Although this constructive communion is a gift of the Holy Spirit, it is concretely realized through our efforts to build community, with ourselves and with others. This spirituality of constructing union implies a readiness to build on common values and to reciprocally die to our individualistic tendencies.

Thus the vocation and mission of the Christian community is to be a dynamic sacrament of communion: an outward sign to the world of God's grace.

In John's Gospel, Jesus says, "Love one another as I have loved you" (John 15:12). The communal nature of Christian discipleship and its mission respond to the deep needs of all men and women who yearn for freedom from loneliness, from alienation from society, from personal isolation, and from a sense of rootlessness and anonymity. The fact that no one can achieve his or her destiny in isolation but only in and with others is a driving force that brings humanity together and leads all people to a dynamic interrelationship which facilitates personal growth.

Trying to be with others in the way of love, however, quickly makes us understand we can only exist together as God's own family. No one can make it on his or her own but only as part of a people who worship the God of love. We realize that the way of love is communal, that loving others as we journey to God is not just an option but rather an integral element of the journey.

This is not a solitary venture, as if each one of us is the point of departure for this journey. Rather, God is the point of departure, and we are being drawn to the life of love not individually but as a people. This is what gives us life as a Church: "We know that we have passed from death to life because we love one another, whoever does not love abides in death" (1 John 3:14).

The Second Vatican Council declared that the Church is "Established by Christ as a fellowship of life, charity and truth" (*Church Today* 45:1). We understand the Church as both a local and a universal reality, but we know that the worldwide community of faith can only be built on the foundations of the local expressions of Church in family, local congregations, and friendship groups.

We build up the way of love at the level of local Church through the development of real and reciprocal relationships, which means we strive to be devoted to the good of others, welcoming them into our lives with Christian hospitality, always showing mutual respect, and taking the necessary risks to try to understand other people's ways and cultures. This initial giving of Christian love is nurturing, strengthening, and hope-filled. It begins with simple gestures of love and concern: "As God's chosen ones, holy and beloved, clothe yourselves with compassion, kindness, humility, meekness, and patience. Bear with one another and, if anyone has a complaint against another, forgive each other" (Colossians 3:12-13).

These basic expressions of community are humanizing, caring, trusting, and supportive. Groups that bear witness to love though their actions toward one another can foster creative tolerance of ambiguity and differences that can lead to the work of world peacemaking. Likewise, genuine groups of mutual support become a model for a fellowship of forgiveness throughout society. Such groups respect members' interdependence and solidarity as they strive together to bear witness to the way of love with mutual inspiration, courage, vitality, and appreciation of each other's talents and charisms.

Communities of love bear witness to a percolating model of Church. Major life-giving values do not filter down from high up in an institutional structure; rather, they percolate up from the base. If we understand the percolating model of the Church from Vatican II, then our concern is that love be lived in the primary, basic, local communities that are the foundation of the Church. In our generation we must live as distinctively Church with creative fidelity and faithful creativity. "Above all, clothe yourselves with love, which binds everything together in perfect harmony" (Colossians 3:14). If we are to look ourselves in the face as disciples today, we must be part of loving communities and only then reach to spread the love of the Lord throughout the world.

There is an intimate connection between our individual growth in faith and love and our growth as communities of love. Yet we often face a rather difficult road in the practice of building loving communities, and we sometimes even end up with "communities" in which people are isolated and anonymous. It is not surprising, then, that the Church feels the need to pray, "Lord, we meet around your table as your family: help us to see that our bitterness is forgotten, our discord is resolved, and our sins are forgiven" (*Psalter*, Week 2, Sunday, Morning Prayer, III).

While it is true that early Christians were known for their fellowship and love, it is not true for us Christians today. In fact, the work of God's love within us is threatened by our lack of reconciliation with one another. Certainly there seems at times more divisiveness than love in us. The strangest thing is that so much of our animosity is over non-essential issues.

Life in the contemporary Church is increasingly a call to reconciliation, which is precisely how Paul viewed the needs of the early Church. He told the rather divisive Corinthian community: "Everything has become new! All this is from God, who reconciled us to himself through Christ, who has given us the ministry of reconciliation; that is, in Christ God was reconciling the world to himself" (2 Corinthians 5:18-19). Everyone who wishes to walk along the way of love must both model reconciliation and proclaim it, aware that unless we exist as a reconciling community we cannot exist as Christians at all. We lose our potential for individual spiritual growth. This reality calls us to rekindle our enthusiasm to search and work for a vision of unity and to rededicate ourselves to acquire skills of communication, community building, understanding, conflict management, and the art of healing divisions and mutual distrust, fostering dialogue, and challenging discrimination.

Nothing takes precedence over reconciliation, not even the outward worship of God (see Matthew 5:23-24). Reconciliation is linked to our humanness and wholeness, and when absent our worship is nothing but empty words. Reconciliation needs honesty, faith, prayer, and the grace of the Lord. It is a total gift of self, total reception of others, and total sharing. It is manifested in forgiveness and produces a communion of peace that prophetically challenges the world to believe. When reconciliation is lost, the community loses its value and meaning; and when we refuse to be reconciled, we destroy the Christian dimension of our own personality. We have witnessed many lost opportunities for reconciliation in our contemporary politics, social life, family life, and Church life.

Every act of reconciliation is liberating and creative, because it is a sharing in the divine life of love. Paul claimed that the whole message of salvation could be summed up in the idea of reconciliation: "In Christ God was reconciling the world to himself...and entrusting the message of reconciliation to us" (2 Corinthians 5:19). This relationship between reconciliation and Christian faith is so intimate that we must recommit ourselves to dialogue that leads to reconciliation. Every situation we deal with in community, including conflict and opposition, can become an opportunity for resurrection, and we grow through such situations as we journey together to greater love.

The challenge to proclaim reconciliation within contemporary Church communities starts by reaching out to those the Church has marginalized or rejected. It means building bridges to people who are more conservative or liberal than we consider ourselves to be. It means listening to what young people have to say, even if it is not "orthodox."

At the local level of Church life, whatever the composition of the group, there are several attitudes that lead toward a reconciling community. First of all we need mutual respect and benevolence towards one another—something so often lacking in our encounters today. Aware that religion is a mystery with few definitive answers, we have to try to understand others' different views and enter into dialogue with them to enrich our own perspective—not to convince others that we are right and they are wrong. This approach should be accompanied by constant self-questioning. It used to go without saying, but recent experience has reminded us that we need to urge believers of all persuasions to avoid deliberate attempts to find fault with others and to follow Christian teaching regarding freedom of conscience.

Christian redemptive love requires risk taking, care for each other, supportiveness, compassion without pity, and love without sentimentality. Maintaining reconciling love is especially difficult in times of transition, when we must enter the suffering of others and work together for a better vision of a loving community that liberates all humans from whatever burdens they endure.

Our yearnings as disciples of Jesus to be in local community are inseparable from our efforts to build community throughout the world. Without the latter, the former would become self-centered and stifled. Without the former, we would become cynical and exhausted.

Local communities can provide intimate experiences of love among family, friends, church, and neighborhood groups. Each of us, seeking to contribute to the way of love, can give greater emphasis to treating others with gentleness, sympathy, serenity, and joy. The way of love should help us be less anxious, more pliant, and able to avoid adversarial roles, even to surrender to others' views, hopes, and dreams: "Rejoice with those who rejoice, weep with those who weep. Live in harmony with one another; do not be haughty, but associate with the lowly; do not claim to be wiser than you are" (Romans 12:15-16).

Such gatherings offer a natural way for people to come together. We can share experiences, achieve personal recognition, find emotional support, and develop enduring friendship. They also provide us a sense of wholeness and coherence through stability and diversity, a sense of control over our lives, and a special place or group we can call our own. For better or worse, community at this level is the future of the Christian community, for there is a dynamic interrelationship between family, friends, congregations, and neighborhood groups, each enriching the other.

Yet while community strategically begins at the grassroots it must percolate through example and testimony up to larger groups of which we are a part. While primary groups, such as the family or the congregation, have more intimacy and spontaneity than larger groups, they are schools of community where we discover and foster many of the skills we need in larger communities. Our dedication to building a local community requires effort to establish a spirit of union and community at civic, work, social, and political levels. These efforts need skill and strategy. Generally this starts with common projects in the area of technical progress but leads to deeper interpersonal relationships, dignity, and mutual respect.

The Church, in its mission of community, becomes a teacher humbly assisting the world in its search for unity. The work of unity is the fundamental mission of the Church. The Church's basic attitude ought to be the establishment of unity at all levels; thus, its mission is an extension of its own inner nature.

The vision of faith that leads to awareness that we are dependent on one another becomes the basis for a world becoming more unified in love. The fact that the Church's inner nature is to be a community and that its mission is to spread the gospel that Jesus brings salvation in community leads to many concrete implications in the way we live individually and together. It calls for listening skills, a spirit of dialogue, collaboration, generosity, and even magnanimity. The spirit of community reminds us that we are all yearning for community and yet all destroying it too—at the same time dedicated and compassionate, but also victims and oppressors. We need training to criticize constructively, to confront with care, and to overcome shared guilt in our pursuit of love and truth.

The spirituality of community building demands inserting ourselves into the paschal mystery—dying to all forms of individualism and particularism, whether as individuals or as groups. After all, Jesus solved the problems of hate with the cross. The death and self-sacrifice that community requires includes the death of all autocratic actions, polarization, bitterness, mutual blame, and judgment. Disciples of Jesus can respond joyfully to tensions and obstacles they encounter, knowing that love proves itself through sacrifice.

Christian community is not inbred, narcissistic, or selfish. It is open to the wider world community and those of other faiths and no faith at all. Therefore, while Christianity has traditionally been mono-cultural, our vision must now include a dedication to multiple cultures and ways of seeing things as part of our vision of the world as it should be.

We Christians must live out our commitment to community, the very nature and mission of the Church, at every level in order to establish the true authority of the Church in the world and reaffirm the confidence and enthusiasm of its believers: "But speaking the truth in love, we must grow up in every way into him who is the head, into Christ, from whom the whole body, joined and knit together by every ligament with which it is equipped, as each part is working properly, promotes the body's growth in building itself up in love" (Ephesians 4:15-16).

QUESTIONS FOR DISCUSSION
FOR PERSONAL REFLECTION ·······································

1. *Name the principal local communities in your life. Do they operate on love and reconciliation? Why or why not? Give examples. What might you do to make these communities more a model of how Christian love operates?*

2. *Have you ever observed love "percolating up"? Tell the story. What caused this to occur? Did you have a part in it? Explain.*

3. *How does community bring the transforming power of Christian love to the world? What is the Church's role in making that happen? What might be your role? Be specific.*

EPILOGUE

Writing an entire book about Christian love has been as difficult as trying to live it. However, this exercise has provided me with a resounding affirmation of its centrality to the Christian message. It challenges every choice we make in our personal and our Church and civic lives.

I believe the awareness of God's revelation in Jesus of Nazareth, the experience of others who have gone before us on this journey, and our own insights into what lies beyond the normal horizons of life are enough to persuade us that love alone offers a clear perspective on the world as it should be. When we look at our world with all its wounds and problems, we see over and over again that it needs a strategy based on community. We Christians can model that strategy, both on the local level and as it percolates up in the greater Church and society.

As we Christians grow in maturity and commitment, this transforming power of Christian love will save the world. This I believe.

Leonard Doohan
Spokane, Washington, and Umbria, Italy

ACKNOWLEDGMENTS

With gratitude to my wife, Helen, for all her help in reading the manuscript and for her many suggestions throughout the writing of this book.

I also thank Gregory F. Augustine Pierce, President and Co-Publisher of ACTA Publications, for his meticulous editing, many helpful suggestions, and constant care in guiding the manuscript to completion. I feel fortunate to have benefitted from his care, skills, and vision.

BOOKS OF RELATED INTEREST

INVITATION TO THE OLD TESTAMENT
INVITATION TO THE NEW TESTAMENT
Alice Camille

Companion books that offer clear, concise, and informative explanations of both the Old and New Testaments. Two separate paperbacks, $9.95 each

THE FORGIVENESS BOOK
Alice Camille and Paul Boudreau

Perhaps the single best explanation of and guide to the Christian approach to forgiveness based on love. Paperback with leatherette cover, $12.95

THE CATHOLIC COMPANION TO MARY
THE CATHOLIC COMPANION TO JESUS
Mary Kathleen Glavich, SND

Two books full of facts, stories, prayers, quotes, places, and pieties about Mary and Jesus. Two separate paperbacks, $9.95 each

RUNNING INTO THE ARMS OF GOD
THE GEOGRAPHY OF GOD'S MERCY
THE LONG YEARNING'S END
by Patrick Hannon, CSC

This trilogy of stories of the presence of God in daily life looks at love-in-action. Three separate paperbacks, $12.95 each

Available from Booksellers or 800-397-2282
www.actapublications.com